MORNINGS
With ABBA

A Reflective Devotional . . .

BECAUSE YOU ARE HIS SONS, GOD SENT THE SPIRIT OF
HIS SON INTO OUR HEARTS, THE SPIRIT WHO CALLS OUT,
"ABBA, FATHER."
GALATIANS 4:6

C.A. GRILL

Mornings With Abba
A Reflective Devotional
by C.A.Grill

Printed in the United States of America.

Edited by Xulon Press.

ISBN 9781498477994

www.xulonpress.com

Dedication

J ustin Grill, whose tiny hand captured my heart for eternal purposes and whose faith encourages me daily.

Adam Grill, who keeps my eyes on Heaven and brings logic and laughter to my life.

Lucas Grill, whose smiles, hugs, and positive outlook on life nourish my soul.

Don Grill, my beloved husband. Thank you for never giving up on me, for being my first Bible teacher, for your constant, consistent walk with the Lord. Thank you for loving me regardless of my behavior and for showing me the meaning of forgiveness. Truly, I now understand the vow, "two shall become one," because of the love you have shown me. I love you heart, mind, soul, and spirit.

Introduction

Some time ago, God impressed it upon my heart that I should write. When God asked this of me, I simply said, "I don't think so . . . I cannot write." After a long period of time and some amazing "God" moments, I came into obedience and agreed. That led me to yet another question: what was I supposed to write? The answer took about one breath, and in that breath I knew it was truly God talking to me for one simple reason: the writing was already done. God was simply asking me to share excerpts from my devotional journals.

My journey began in 1979. I accepted Christ in the recovery room after giving birth to our first son, Justin. At this point, I knew *how* to accept Christ, but it was Justin's tiny hand wrapped around my finger that brought me to Him. Following my acceptance of Jesus Christ, it was under the tutelage of Pastor Bob Wilbur that my walk with Jesus was given wings. I was learning quickly and I was walking toward righteousness, finding everything about the Lord amazing! I then learned the hard way that there are many tests and temptations along the way, and it still saddens me to say that at times I have utterly failed.

In 1998, I was given the devotional *Experiencing GOD, Knowing And Doing The Will Of God* by Richard T. Blackaby & Claude V. King. This was the beginning of falling head over heels in love with my God and Savior Jesus. It was during this time that I realized the difference between a "head knowledge" belief in Christ and the soul deep love relationship that follows when one accepts the "Lordship of Christ." It was also during this time that I began writing a love letter to my Lord every morning. Contained in these pages are some of those love letters to my Lord.

In August of 2001, I attended a prayer school. It was during this week that again I was transformed with an even deeper love and understanding of "walking with Christ." I learned the meaning of moving from soul-deep living into being captured by the profound gift of the Holy Spirit living within me.

The title of this book and my use of the name "Abba," came from a trip to the Holy Land many years ago. I had been praying that God would give me a more intimate name for Him because I loved Him so deeply. I had always called my own father "daddy"; therefore, I did not feel right using this name for God. Our Israeli guide, Isaac, said to one of our boys, "Ask your Abba," which is Hebrew for daddy. I knew at that moment that I had found the name for my Lord. It was a natural fit for me to subsequently call this journal, *Mornings with Abba.*

I believe that Abba's goal in having me share this with you is twofold. First, to see that a deeply personal and loving relationship with the Him is possible, and secondly, it is what we were created for!

Approaching Abba

Each of us is an ordinary person made extraordinary by Jesus alone. If you desire to hear the words, "well done good and faithful servant," then you must take a first step, followed by another and another. When we truly grasp the wonder of the God we serve, we, too, can be transformed and positively impact our world for eternity, by accepting Jesus as our Lord and Savior.

Our eternal citizenship is based on Jesus and Jesus alone.

Consider these verses:

Romans 6:23 states, *For the wages of sin is death, but the gift of God is eternal life in Christ Jesus our Lord.*

Scripture also states, *"The man who says, 'I know him,' but does not do what he commands is a liar, and the truth is not in him. But if anyone obeys his word, God's love is truly made complete in him. This is how we are in him: Whoever claims to live in him must walk as Jesus did"* (1 John 2:4–5).

In James 2: 22–24, 26, this truth is revealed: *"You see that his faith and his actions were working together, and his faith was made complete by what he did. And the scripture was fulfilled that says, 'Abraham believed God, and it was credited to him as righteousness,' and he was called God's friend. You see that a person is justified by what he does and not by faith alone. As the body without spirit is dead, so faith without deeds is dead."* The faith that is spoken of here is faith in Jesus Christ.

It also states in Romans 10:9–10 *"That if you confess with your mouth, 'Jesus is Lord,' and believe in your heart that God raised him from the dead, you will be saved. For it is with your heart that you believe and are justified, and it is with your mouth that you confess and are saved."*

Finally, *"The good man brings good things out of the good stored up in his heart, and the evil man evil things out of the evil stored up in his heart. For out of the overflow of his heart his mouth speaks"* (Luke 6:45).

Make today your "first step" and allow God to transform your life to one that He will bless forever.

Let's begin with an exercise on relationship building . . .

I have an assignment for you. Sit back and think about a person you love. In the space provided, answer the following questions.

1. What makes this person special?

2. Why do you love him/her?

3. Could you lose your love for him/her? If so, how and why?

4. Do you enjoy spending time with this person? Why?

5. Do you believe he/she enjoys spending time with you? Why?

6. Could you have this special loving relationship without investing time into it?

7. Can you think of any loving relationship that does not require time in order to strengthen it and to create a

lasting bond? If you are separated from this person because of the military or an assignment far from home, how does the lack of time spent with him/her affect your relationship? How do you overcome it?

How does this apply to Abba?

Now, let's change gears a bit. I assume that most of your responses to the questions have painted a picture that looks like this:

TIME INVESTED = DEPTH OF RELATIONSHIP

If you agree with this assumption, do you believe that it is any different with God, Jesus, and the Holy Spirit? Do you believe this equation?

TIME INVESTED + FOCUSED ATTENTION = DEPTH OF RELATIONSHIP WITH GOD

Consider these questions . . .

1. Do you believe that you can have a close relationship with Jesus on a personal level without the investment of time? With God? With the Holy Spirit?

2. If you spent Sunday morning with your loved one and ignored him/her for the remainder of the week, how long do you think the relationship would remain strong? What if you didn't even bother with Sunday morning?

3. How strong would the relationship be if you talked to the person you love only when trouble was brewing? When you were extremely happy? When you really needed something?

In light of your answers, why do we think that bullet prayers, thanks or occasional requests of God are enough? The picture I am painting by the questions you have answered is obvious. Spending time with God is crucial to maintaining a right relationship with Him . . . and getting to know Him as Abba.

Steps to a successful journey . . .

1. Try your best to get to bed at a decent time so that you will be prepared to rise early enough to spend at least thirty minutes with God. If your kids are up by 6:00, plan to get up at 5:30.

2. Set a schedule and stick to it. Mornings were best for me! When I began my journey, I noted that the people who truly walked closely with the Lord—chose to start their day with Him. Always remember: this is the model that Jesus taught us. (Read the book of Luke, note the time Jesus prayed . . . consistently.)

3. Buy a Bible, such as the Life Application Bible, with big margins (for taking notes) and with good commentary explaining difficult passages. You will also need a highlighter and a pen; keep them with this journal.

4. Choose a spot in your house where you can be *alone* early in the morning. This will become your special place to meet with the Lord. Keep all of your supplies there. (I have a small bag next to my chair that contains everything I need. I take the bag with me even when I travel.)

5. Have you ever heard the phrase "half-hearted?" Well, there will be days when you really won't want to get up and you really won't want to read, study or pray. **Do It Anyway!** Make this a habit like brushing your teeth, showering or having a cup of coffee when you wake. This must become a *part* of your routine without becoming **routine**. If you miss a few days,

don't beat yourself up or give up. Get back on track and start again.

6. If you have a prolonged period when you feel as if you are "faking it," ask God to search your heart for a wrong motive, hidden sin, wrong thinking or outright disobedience. Confess it, as it is revealed, and you will quickly return to a oneness with Him! Remember that sometimes God is silent, and it may have nothing to do with the condition of your heart. It may be His way of allowing you time to see things from a new or different perspective.

These are the steps I have developed to guide my Mornings with Abba

1. I address The Holy Trinity intimately and in all their Biblical forms. Abba, God the Father, Jesus (God the Son), and The Holy Spirit.

2. I put on my armor as described in Ephesians 6:10–18. As Christians, we must be battle ready each and every day. Without our armor we are an easy target for the enemy. Each piece of armor strengthens us in a different manner and therefore, we should not fail to dress with care each morning in order to be fully clothed in Christ's Righteousness.

3. I always ask for forgiveness . . . there are days that this happens at different times for me, but it always comes up, God is faithful that way. He wants us to be honest with ourselves and with Him!

4. I read Scripture (sometimes just a verse or two and at other times several passages).

5. I praise God.

6. I pray through specific requests on my list of family, friends and issues.

7. I journal whatever is on my heart. I make it a love letter, and sign it. You will notice that my journaling time is simply a thought stream which follows (loosely) the conversation I am having with the Lord. Remember, that these entries are a snapshot of the time I spend with the Lord. Much of what we discuss never makes it into print.

8. I spend the remaining time imagining that Jesus is in the chair next to me and I ask Him what he needs to talk to me about. This is a critical and very revealing time—don't miss out on this step!

The Journey Begins . . .

If you decide to take this journey of devotional journaling it will take you about three months. The use of my daily entries—I believe—is for you to have jumping off points and to discover that there is nothing off limits in your time with the Lord. Sometimes in the beginning of my journey I had a hard time simply starting the conversation. I hope this journal helps you conquer that issue. At first, perhaps for a week or two, allow Him to touch you each morning and embrace you with His unfailing love.

As I have followed these steps faithfully over the years I have become a new person in Christ; I am completely in love with my Lord, Savior, and Creator God!

Keep your heart with all diligence, for out of it spring the issues of life.
Proverbs 4:23

Good Morning, Abba, Jesus, Holy Spirit,

It is my desire to fill the pages of this journal with love letters to you. I want to fall in love with you as completely as is humanly possible. Please, Abba God, honor this prayer. I know You are in control, and that is a comfort to me. Teach me to be obedient today and always. Show me how to be the daughter You created me to be, remind me I am of royal blood now, and, therefore, I must act with dignity, truth, and honor. Forgive me when I fail You, and please, Savior Jesus, intercede for me. Wash me clean each day, and teach me your ways. As I strive to live my life in a way that honors You, bless my efforts, I pray. Thank you for the gifts You have given me, infuse my spirit with the fact that You Holy Spirit will give me the gifts of Your bounty as I have need . . . if I only ask. Give me the strength to handle the negative happenings in my days.

Abba, give me a fresh outlook, allow me to see things Your way. Grow within my soul a longing, desire, and ability to go to the depths of my being with You! To You and You alone I give praise and honor this day.

I love You so.

Thoughts to Ponder

1. What are the critical things you need to work on?

2. Do you desire to go into the depths with God?

At daybreak Jesus went out to a solitary place.
Luke 4:42

Good Morning, Abba, Jesus, Holy Spirit,

Jesus, I have been thinking about Your prayer life and realizing that every single move You made was dictated by what You heard during Your prayer time with Abba. You did not sleep in, because you were up late or had a rough previous day, You never said, I think I will just roll over to catch a few extra winks and catch a few seconds with Abba on my way out to meet the man possessed by demons. Clearly, just as meeting a man possessed would not have gone well unprepared, my life does not go well when I am unprepared. At daybreak You got up and spent time with Abba. Is it really that much for me to do likewise?

Clearly You want my devotion to You and You alone, a new way, a changed heart, and an understanding of what it is you want, my devotion to You and You alone. It isn't service, promises or anything I could ever "DO." You simply want me to be fully devoted to You. I pray that You will allow our times together to be times of teaching and learning how to order my days in order to bring You glory. Holy Spirit, please guide every moment of my life so that the love of Jesus will shine through me.

The hardest part of living in this world is living consistently for you, Abba. It is so easy to fall prey to this world and its standards. Help me to live a pure, consecrated life in You. My desire is that *only* You, Jesus, will shine through me. Abba, show me every step I must take to allow this prayer to become a reality. I pray that You will continue to bless my family, our churches, missionaries, and believers the world over in our service for You.

I love You so,

Thoughts to Ponder

1. Are you willing to forgo sleep for a deeper relationship with God?

2. Do you need to re-order your days? Your time?

For where your treasure is, there your heart will be also.

Matthew 6:21

Good Morning Abba, Jesus, Holy Spirit,

My Treasure is in YOU! You know me so well. You and You alone knit me together in Mamma's womb. How incredible that You made me just as You wanted me to be. Every nook and cranny of who I am was designed by You . . . The Master of Design. You are magnificent in every way, and I praise You, Abba.

Please forgive me for my sins. Jesus, it is hard for me to realize that my sin nailed YOU to the cross. The perfect Son of God Most High went willingly to the cross for me. Your sacrifice was horrible, yet beautiful at the same time. The selflessness of Your gift is truly remarkable. There are no human words that could ever truly define what You did. Holy Spirit, it says in Scripture that You will pray for me when words fail me, and I ask You this day to pray a prayer of thanksgiving on my behalf to Jesus, my beloved Savior.

Abba, mold me, make me into a child that will bring honor and glory to Your Kingdom forever. Bless every day of my life with Your perfect guidance. Give me extraordinary wisdom to serve You by serving my brothers and sisters as well as those who have not yet met You. Show me each step that I must take to grow closer to You. Create in me a clean heart that will be infectious to others.

I do love You so . . .

Thoughts to Ponder

1. Does your life reflect someone that is moldable or do you have a rigidity of thought that makes change difficult?

2. What do you spend the majority of your time thinking about?

Ask and it will be given to you. Seek and you will find.
Knock and it will be opened to you.
Matthew 7:7

Good Morning, Abba, Jesus, Holy Spirit,

As I sit here in a warm home, the beauty of nature surrounding me, soft music playing, a cup of coffee beside me and YOU ever present with me, I ask YOU, could I ever count the blessings of living life with You? Of course I know the answer to that question is NEVER . . . but I would like to spend my life trying (at the very least) to thank You for them.

Asking is an interesting endeavor when it comes to YOU. I believe there is far more to the "ask" than we could ever realize. You are certainly not the "Shell Answer Man" nor are You a God that gives frivolously and with total abandon from the human perspective. If You gave without regard to what is good for me . . . for us individually and collectively then we would be spoiled and entitled and that is an ugly thing indeed. Frankly, our country is presently on a collision course with entitlement gone awry. However, when we ask with a right heart, YOU give generously and You give what we truly need, not what we necessarily want.

Thank You, my Holy, True, and Righteous Abba God! Jesus, once again I am at a loss for how to thank You for being my Savior, my teacher, my brother and my friend. Thank You for helping me to see truth and righteousness, for never giving up on me, and for reminding me daily that You are real and present in my life. I am grateful to You for giving us Your plan of salvation and for seeking me to belong to You and Your family of believers.

Abba, soften the hearts of my family and friends who don't know You. Allow me to be a light in their lives that daily shows them who You are. Please shine through me. When I stumble and totally blow it, please keep me from harming others.

I love You so, and I ask that this day be one of Kingdom-building potential.

Love & Thanks . . .

Thoughts to Ponder

1. Do you ask with right motives?

2. Do you believe that you are entitled to receive the answers you want from God?

No good tree bears bad fruit, nor does a bad tree bear good fruit. Each tree is recognized by it's own fruit.
Luke 6: 43–44

Abba, I love You,

Abba, Jesus, Spirit, on this beautiful morning with the splendor of Your creation surrounding me I wonder . . . what must Heaven be like? More wondrous than our imaginations can fathom, and as You know I have a vivid imagination! Living in Michigan makes me extremely grateful for the sunshine, thank YOU! Jesus, I am so thankful that You shine within me each and every day of the year.

Today is a new day of life and opportunity. This can be a day of bearing good fruit or bad. It is truly my desire to be known by my good fruit. Abba, I suppose that I need to ask myself hard questions such as; do I lack patience, am I kind, would others say I am filled with joy, do I love everyone or only those that are easy to love? The answer is obvious—not always—so Abba, I ask that You fill me to overflowing with; peace, love, joy, patience, kindness, faithfulness, gentleness, and self-control. Teach me how to be a bearer of good fruit every moment of every day.

For those who are searching for You this day, I ask that You soften, convict, and clear up their confusion caused by living on a fallen and hurting planet. Show them clearly which of their thoughts are right concerning who You are and what You are . . . and are not. It is the enemy who confuses and deceives, and I ask that You make that obvious this day by opening their eyes and ears to the Truth.

Give me Spiritual eyes to see and Spiritual ears to hear clearly the way to "bear good fruit," I pray in You, Jesus.

I love You . . .

Thoughts to Ponder

1. If you were to take each fruit of the Spirit and truly look for it in your life, what would you see?

2. Where is it easy for you to be a bearer of good fruit? Where is it hard?

A desire accomplished is sweet to the soul.
Proverbs 13:19

Good Morning, Abba, Jesus, Holy Spirit,

It brings me such joy to do my tasks as if I am doing them for You. I desire to become a daughter who will one day . . . hear You say . . ." Well done good and faithful servant." Truly, Your ways are not our ways and it is this fact that helps spur me on to love and good deeds! My story is one of many starts and stops, failures and some successes in this walk with YOU. This will be a story of victory . . . if in the end it brings glory to YOU alone. Everyone who has come to know You lives out a unique and wonder-filled story of redemption. Life is never the same once we meet the One True Living God.

Forgive me for lost opportunities to plant seeds. Forgive me when I am not being sensitive to Your instruction. Forgive me, Jesus, for so many missed chances. More and more each day, I understand Paul's prayer concerning doing the very thing he does not want to do. Why are we such weak-minded people? Use me in spite of my weakness, I pray.

This day, I ask that You give me a bold Spirit for Your purposes.

With love . . .

Thoughts to Ponder

1. We each have areas of life that are hard for us, how are you finding victory in your "hard places"?

2. Can you sense when the Holy Spirit is prompting you to plant a seed with someone? If so, what stops you from sharing your seeds of hope? Are you ready to ask the Holy Spirit to give you eyes to see?

Let everything that has breath praise the Lord.
Psalm 150:6

Good Morning, Abba, Jesus, Holy Spirit,

As I sit here with You so early in the morning with only the with the hush of morning as our companion, I feel so blessed, loved, and cared for. Thank You, Abba, for the blessings You have so richly given to me. I thank You for the peace that I have, the inner joy, the gladness of heart and spirit. All of the wonders of this most blessed life are from You and You alone.

My God, my Savior, my first love. You are the Master of my soul, the giver of good things, and the just judge of all I do. I humbly ask that You accept me one day into Your Heavenly Kingdom scrubbed clean by the sacrifice of my Savior.

Jesus, I have been thinking about You being fully God and fully man . . . You were fully man, and yet You alone remained perfect . . . never sinning! That will always be a huge triumph in my heart and mind. You focused so completely on Your mission that even in Your full humanity You were able to conquer sin. Thank You for staying the course and never losing sight of Your purpose. You were the ultimate role model for each of us, reminding us that every action, thought, and deed must be captured for Kingdom purpose if we are to be role models for our children.

My heart soars with the hope I find in You, my Lord and my Savior . . . also my Friend. Give me courage, strength, boldness and compassion for the lost and hurting of our world. To You I give honor and praise this day.

Love and honor to You . . .

Thoughts to Ponder

1. Our 'human nature' often distracts us from our mission, so maintaining focus is critical. What do you do to remain focused in the fray of living?

2. Jesus was always in communication with His Father as it was in essence, His way of life. Is it yours? Is the Lord Your front line of defense?

Your hands have made me and fashioned me. Give me understanding, that I may learn Your commandments.
Psalms 119:73

Good Morning, Abba, Jesus, Holy Spirit,

Abba, does this journal reflect the inner workings of my relationship with You . . . and the millions of conversations in-between my thought streams that make it onto paper? I was thinking about how long my journals would be if I wrote it all down. I am thick headed at times and I need You to give me understanding so I properly learn YOUR commandments and YOUR ways . . . that takes me a long time. So while these letters are just snapshots of our conversations, they do honestly reflect what we talk about.

Please guide my thoughts, prayers, reading, and learning to bring about answers to the questions and yearnings of my heart. May my heart be one devoted to You, my Master and my Maker.

Love to Heaven this day . . .

Thoughts to Ponder

1. God's Word is living and active and should create in us a desire to learn more, pray more and want more of Jesus! Is this true for you? If not what do you think is missing to make this true?

2. Do you think that memorizing God's commandments and the teachings of Jesus make a difference?

You shall love the Lord your God with all your heart,
with all your soul, with all your strength, and with all
your mind, and your neighbor as yourself.
Luke 10:27

Good Morning, Abba, Jesus, Spirit,

Ezekiel chapter 16 is shocking! It is a clear picture of the USA! Abba, please hear the cry of the faithful remnant, and turn this nation back to You before it is too late. Spirit, convict Christians to get back to Your calling. We are supposed to be the ones making disciples of all nations, and we can't (or won't) even disciple our own nation!

When I consider Luke 10:27 Abba, isn't it the answer to the woes we face? It seems we have skipped the first part of the verse because if we loved You with all of our heart, soul and strength we would embrace Your Word and Your Ways! Today, many who claim to be Christians pick and choose what they like out of the Bible and dismiss the rest as cultural or applicable to that time in history. This makes Your Word an interesting novel to them . . . not the living breathing work of the Holy Trinity. Additionally, I think we have become confused. We have decided that loving our neighbor is akin to accepting everything and anything our 'neighbor' does. And some even believe that we must embrace whatever they do! Doing anything less is intolerant! See Abba, I think we are called to be intolerant of sin. What has happened to the concept of loving the sinner, but hating the sin? I hate my sin! It disgusts me that there are things that still entangle me . . . but I don't hate myself. Actually I clearly love myself and I take great care of myself. Every day I shower, put on clothes, eat, do things I like to do, enjoy friendships, I love and I am loved . . . but I still hate my sin. There is one thing that is pretty important here . . . To write off others because of their sin is wrong. After all Jesus . . . sinners are the people You hung out with!

If we turn back to You and love You with all of our heart, soul and strength, and embrace Your Word and Your Ways as the only way . . . then wouldn't we truly love our neighbors . . . and perhaps . . . just perhaps we would see our nation restored to one that honors YOU.

Forgive us, Abba. In Your name, Jesus, I ask that You show us the way to do our part . . . all of us who truly care about the future of this nation. Make me, mold me, and use me each day to be a Kingdom builder. Let me be ever mindful of the result of disobedience in all things, even the small stuff! Change the hearts of families, friends, and entire communities. Bring this nation into communion with You once again. Give us hearts for Your will alone, and create Spirit-filled believers to set this nation afire.

To You and You alone will the glory and praise belong. In humble love and adoration . . .

Thoughts to Ponder

1. What comes to mind when you consider the word intolerant?

2. Contrast the thoughts and actions of a people-pleaser vs. a God-pleaser . . .

I am your servant; give me discernment that I may
understand your statues.
Psalm 119:125

Good Morning, Abba, Jesus, Spirit of the Holy God,

Today I choose to lose my fear of what You may ask of me. You are mighty in power and more than able to accomplish anything You ask of me. Thank You for using me for Your purpose. I love the way You take me step by step. You never give me more than I am ready to handle. Sometimes I think it is too much, but You know my limits better than I do.

Discernment is interesting to be sure. Often, I feel like I sense things about total strangers and I feel a strong urgency to pray for them but other times I feel like You ask me to ask them if I can help them and I chicken out. There are times Abba that I can feel their sorrow, anger, or fear. When I sense You asking me to do more, please show me what I am supposed to do and give me the courage to follow through!

You are so good to me, Abba. I never cease to be amazed by You! Show me the way to completely "die to self," that I may totally live for You. Abba, place in my path those to whom I may minister by Your power and saving grace. Jesus and Holy Spirit . . . create in me a sensitivity that transcends human understanding. I desire to see, hear, speak, and touch with Spiritual eyes, ears, lips, and hands. I pray You will make it so.

I love You so.

Thoughts to Ponder

1. Do you trust in your discernment, believing that it is God prompting you?

2. Do you think that knowing the Word of God is a part of strong discernment?

Cast your burden on the LORD, and He shall sustain you; He shall never permit the righteous to be moved.
Psalm 55:22

Good Morning, Abba, Jesus and Gracious Spirit,

Oh, how You care for me! You pamper me like a princess. I am the daughter of the One True King, and I feel like royalty! I am surrounded by Your riches. Thank You for the work You have done in my soul.

Abba, I have far to go before truly having a heart like the Lion of Judah. I love this mind picture of You Jesus, it evokes within me the passion and courage we are to possess having been created in Your image. Courage is a trait that would change our world for YOU. To stand for Your Word and righteousness regardless of the consequences . . . well that is the stuff of martyrdom and takes tremendous passion and courage. It is quite the narrow path You ask of us and so I ask that You keep me from slipping off one side into weakness or the other side into becoming complacent. I ask that when my time comes to be courageous for You that I would find Your strength within me to stand strong. I praise You alone for this humbling honor and privilege of being a daughter of the King. I know that no one comes to You, that You did not seek first, and I thank You for seeking me.

The peace that is inside of me is so complete that it can only come from You. I desire at last to be used by You every minute of each day. I desire to fall into bed each night with a "holy tired" feeling that brings me to a peaceful sleep protected by Your angels. Help me to obey in all things that I may be pleasing to You.

Love and kisses . . .

Thoughts to Ponder

1. Do you tend toward a lack of courage or passion? What will it take to change that tendency?

2. The armor of God is the only way to stand strong, do you wear it daily?

But the fruit of the Spirit is love, joy, peace, long-suffering, kindness, goodness, faithfulness, gentleness, self-control. Against such things there is no law.
Galatians 5:22–23

Good Morning, My King and Savior,

Abba, I feel a distance between us this morning. I know that distance is a result of sin, it always is. Spirit, point out to me my sin or wrong thinking so that I will see truth, and repent of whatever this is.

Your word convicts me each day. It only takes one verse for me to see a new area that requires attention in my life! I certainly do have room for improvement in all areas; yet, I don't become discouraged because I trust that You will get me to where You want me to be by the end of my race.

The fruit of the Spirit . . . Your Spirit . . . that one pesky fruit called self-control; that's a tough one for me because I know it is not just about growing my personal grove of fruit to enjoy. That fruit is to be used for the benefit of others. The goal would be for others to see Your fruit growing and flourishing abundantly within me causing others to desire the same . . . thereby bringing Glory to You!

Thank You for showing me that my lack of self-control will lead to distance between us. Remind me that distance grows more easily than closeness. Help me to focus on my witness when I am about to say or do something I shouldn't. Never let me lose sight of the fact that You and You alone are the answer to all things.

Abba, Jesus, Holy Spirit, create in me a clean heart and renew a right spirit within me.

I love You so.

Thoughts to Ponder

1. Is there any fruit that is lacking in you? What will you do about it?

2. Do you think you are hard on yourself in regard to sin or do you give yourself a pass on a lot of sin? What keeps us separated from God?

*Then they said to Him, "What shall we do, that we
may work the works of God?" Jesus answered and
said to them, "This is the work of God that you believe
in Him whom He sent."*
John 6:28–29

Good Morning, Abba, Jesus, Holy Spirit,

Thank You, Abba, for keeping this family safe from the dozens and dozens of things we never even realized were a danger to us. You protect us from so much without our conscious knowledge of these events. Could we live through even one day without Your protection?

You are such a great and mighty God, worthy of all my praise and worship. I have moments when I wonder how it is possible that You do it all. Surely this world is too big to care for. Then, of course, I remember You are God and capable of all things.

I thank You this day by kneeling before You in my heart, bowing my head and saying . . . well, saying nothing because there are no words that can express the deepness of my reverence for You. Holy Spirit, speak on my behalf, I pray.

Sometimes I feel as if my sins are piled high, and then I remember one power-filled word: forgiven. I am forgiven by You, amazing God, amazing Grace, amazing Savior!

Abba, give me more opportunities to share my faith with others. My desire is to do good for You all the days of my life. You are a glorious King, and I will love You all the days left to me on this earth. Bless me with the gifts of Your Spirit that I need in each moment because You alone know me best. I humbly ask to serve You this day.

I love You so much.

Thoughts to Ponder

1. Do you take time to bask in the glory of God?

2. What keeps you from sharing your love for God with others?

*"Refrain from anger and turn from wrath; do not fret—
it leads only to evil. For evil men will be cut off, but
those who hope in the LORD will inherit the land."*
Psalm 37:8–9

Good Morning, Abba, Jesus, Holy Spirit,

Thank You for giving me direction yesterday! Thank You for ever providing me with Your holy guidance. Today I feel weary of the battle and I think I am truly angry. I would like to write a book called, *Do Nice Guys Go To Heaven?* I am just so tired of hearing that a loving God would not put a nice guy in hell. It does not seem to matter that the very same nice guy rejected Your son, denied Your existence, made fun of Your followers and/or denied the truth of Your Holy Word. What people tell me is that all that matters is that "the person in question" never did anything "that bad" . . . thereby earning the right to entrance into Heaven. That is really messed up theology in my opinion. Nothing we do or don't do *earns* a ticket into Heaven. Accepting the sacrifice of Jesus is the only way, but I guess that "appears" to lack the tolerance everyone is so fond of these days.

Abba, please guard my heart and mind against evil and the lies it speaks. Fill me with Your Holy Spirit so that I will speak truth in LOVE, not anger. Forgive me, Father, for this frustration I am feeling. Frustration will accomplish nothing; it will only harm my witness. Give me the strength to speak truth and stop me from speaking when I may do harm. In Jesus' Name I pray.

Love . . .

Thoughts to Ponder

1. Do you ever have a righteous anger about the truth in God's Word?

2. How do you handle situations where you are all alone in your beliefs and you feel like others are ganging up on you?

*"We loved you so much that we were delighted to
share with you not only the gospel of God but our
lives as well, because you had become so dear to us."*
I Thessalonians 2:8

Good Morning, Abba, Jesus, Holy Spirit of God,

Self-less-ness. What exactly does this mean, Father? It personifies Jesus, I realize this, but practically speaking how does this play out in my life? I am willing to give to the point that remains in my comfort zone, but am I truly willing to go beyond? Are *all* people truly dear to me?

What is my truth check? . . . Jesus is . . . always! When Jesus was tired, He got up earlier and prayed longer . . . I sleep. When people needed more of Him, He gave . . . I go home. When all went against Him, He cried out to His Father . . . I look for the door.

Esther had the character of Jesus. Here was a young woman who could have whined, given up or said, "choose someone else" . . . but she didn't . . . she gave it all. She left her only family and had her virginity taken with no guarantee of marriage or happiness. She simply obeyed with incredible grace. The result was a life used by God to save the lineage of Jesus. Esther exudes self-less-ness. Esther is an example for all of us to follow. Choices are about doing the right thing regard-less of the circumstances we may find ourselves in.

Father, it is my desire to be filled with your desire for me . . . to live a self-less life. I am not certain I do right now. It seems like I want to choose when to be self-less. Help me to have more of You and less of me, and forgive me for this humbling realization. To You alone I give praises for pointing this out to me this day.

I love You so much.

Thoughts to Ponder

1. What does stepping out of your comfort zone look like for you?

2. When considering the selfless nature of Esther or Caleb what speaks to you the most?

*I sought the LORD, and He heard me, and delivered
me from all my fears.
Psalm 34:4*

Good Morning, Abba, Jesus, Holy Spirit,

Can words ever express Your wonder? Is it even possible to grasp the heart of You? The light You bring to me shines with a brilliance that is beyond description, and I am awed by You once again.

In all things may I be a light that shines forth. I love You, and I do want to carry through on the desires of Your heart for my life's work. Create in me a Spirit so sensitive to Your calling that all else fades away. Freshen me; fill me; capture my heart, mind and soul; and never let me go.

Today will be an opportunity to shine. Give me a bold, true witness, I pray. Let Your children be power-filled this day. Bring seekers ever closer to accepting You, my Sweet Savior Jesus. Let the time for reaping a harvest begin.

I love You so; come soon . . .

Thoughts to Ponder

1. How often do you sit in awe of God?

2. Today, spend time asking God to capture your heart. At the end of the day answer this . . . what happened to my fears?

*"It is the Spirit who gives life; the flesh profits nothing.
The words that I speak to you are spirit, and they are life."
John 6:63*

Good Morning, Holy Father, my Savior, Gracious Spirit,
I praise You for how truly awesome You are. Your wonder is so huge that I cannot comprehend it. You alone inspire me through Your Spirit and wisdom. I come humbly into Your magnificent presence praising and thanking You.

Abba, where are our elders? Where are the Caleb's and those we need to listen to and learn from? It is wisdom we need that has been developed from a long righteous walk with You . . . a walk filled with Spirit giving life and vitality. Even though I still have so far to go to walk well with YOU . . . and I still have more questions than answers, I am willing to take the time to listen and become an elder for Your purposes. Show me how to become an elder . . . unworthy as I am. I will strive to listen well as You reveal Your heart.

I love You more than any other . . . Holy Trinity make this an absolute truth in me. Would others see me as loving You more than any other? You are more precious to me than money, things, even family; and I do love them dearly. You are my inspiration, the song in my heart, my encouragement, my first love. I long to be enfolded in Your loving arms, to praise You with the saints, to bow before You, Mighty King. Jesus, Prince of Peace, I long to see You coming in Your splendor.

Come soon, Lord Jesus . . .

Thoughts to Ponder

1. In this day we live in, elders are not as respected as they once were—let's say—as little as 40 years ago. If you are an elder how do you feel about this fact? Are there things you can do to change this? If you are young do you think that perhaps you could listen to the heart of your elders and find the pearls of wisdom that they may possess?

2. If you are an elder what are you doing for the Kingdom? Caleb was in his 80's and going strong for Kingdom purposes. What are you doing?

"I will extol You, my God, O King; and I will bless your name forever and ever. Every day I will bless You, and I will praise Your name forever and ever."
Psalm 145:1–2

Good Morning, Abba, Jesus, Spirit,

Oh, how I love You and the fragrance of Your Spirit. Perfect and Holy, true and just . . . the essence of You. Is there anything I could offer that could bless You my God of Holy righteousness? How can I possibly return anything to You, a perfect God? There is nothing I can offer because YOU are the only true Giver-of good gifts. You are strength, I am weakness, You are truth, I am not. You are Creator of all, I am but a tiny part of Your creation . . . a created being, flawed by original sin and the stench of living on a fallen and dying planet deceived by darkness. However, Abba, it is because I am created by You, wooed by Your Spirit, commissioned by Your Son that I am able to give You the one thing all creation can give back, my praise for; Your Glory, Your Victory over sin and death, Your work in our lives, and most of all for giving us the very heart we praise You with. What joy!

In my joy there is also heartache, Abba. The souls of the lost and dying that have never met You cry out to me. I see them drowning, yet they don't see or sense their danger! Open their hearts; soften them to Your truth, Jesus. They have been deceived by this evil world. Please give them one more chance to turn to You.

You are the Rock of my salvation. Show the lost that You want to be their Rock as well. Shine through me so brightly that they cannot miss the reality of You and Your mighty love. Please, never allow me to turn from the lost with a calloused heart. Create in me a powerful witness, I pray.

I love You . . .

Thoughts to Ponder

1. Have you ever spent time considering the fact that we are commissioned by Jesus Christ to reach the lost?

2. What is a step you can take today to live begin living out the Great Commission?

A wife of noble character who can find?
She is worth far more than rubies.
Proverbs 31:10

Good Morning, Father, Son, Holy Spirit of God,

I relish being in Your presence, Lord. When I am upset it is soothing for me to sit and just know that You are with me. Jesus, You spent hours alone with the Father, and I think that is truly the key to this walk with You. While the world sleeps, I fall deeper in love with You. I love You so!

There is a rather difficult behavior of mine that I need You to teach me how to overcome. Paul said that it troubled him that he was prone to do the very thing he did not want to do. Your Bible is amazing . . . I have yet to find a struggle of mine that I cannot find the answer to in Your Word, and today this sums up exactly what I am struggling with. When I am here with You, life is so easy, it is just me (flawed of course) and You . . . Profound and Perfect in every way. However, the day eventually begins with people and it gets so ridiculously hard to be like YOU. I say crabby things to my dearly loved husband and as You well know I don't think he is exactly singing the Proverbs 31 woman praises about me. How is it possible that I could love someone so much and then get so crosswise with him? Half of the time I just want to be alone so that I don't say or do the wrong thing. I know that becoming a sequestered hobbit is not what You ask of us, we are supposed to be acting like YOU in every part of our life. I love being here with You, it is the living it with others . . . that is the tough part for me. I want to be the person I am in my heart, all of the time. Because truly . . . I want to be a loving and patient person all of the time. I want to exude YOU to everyone, but the truth is I don't always or even close to always. Yes, Abba, I am hard on myself, but I need to be because if I give myself a pass on poor behavior one day it becomes a pattern pretty quickly. I desire to change this within me and that is my prayer. Teach me Abba, Jesus, Holy Spirit . . .

Abba, please continue to mold me into a wife, mother, and grandmother who brings honor to You and to my family. I desire to be a Proverbs 31 woman. Help me to walk more closely with You each day. Teach me how to love You more completely and how to honor You every moment. To You, Sovereign Lord, I give my praises.

I love You . . .

Thoughts to Ponder

1. Do you have behaviors that are less than God honoring? Have you asked our Conqueror Jesus to help
   you overcome these behaviors?

2. This question is for men only . . . The Bible teaches
   that you are to love your wife as yourself, how are
   you doing with this command?

*For the LORD takes pleasure in His people; He will
beautify the humble with salvation.
Psalm 149:4*

Good Morning, Father God, Jesus my brother, Spirit within,

Thank You for good gifts. Teach me to use the gifts You have given me with grace and humility. Remind me that they are *good gifts* from You to be used with joy and servanthood! Sometimes I think I am truly an odd duck because I am totally Mary every morning sitting here with YOU. Once the day starts, look out! My Martha heart takes the reigns of wanting things to be so perfect for my family. I become this crazy doer of, cooking, sewing, arranging, as my Mary heart fades to the background.

You gave me this joy for cooking and all thing domestic, so I know it is not a bad thing and I do enjoy it so much. However, please teach me to rein in the "Martha" and to let loose the "Mary" more often. In Luke 10: 38–42, You tell my story. What a life lesson for me. I can just hear Jesus lovingly chuckling to himself, "Martha, Martha, big heart, short fuse!" I like the "big heart" part, but I really want to serve You with a Mary attitude minus the short fuse! Remind me to cook with my hands but sit at Your feet in my heart. It isn't honoring You if I get an attitude in the process!

Oh, Lord, I love You dearly. I wish I had different words to express the depth of my love for You. The English language just does not have enough words to explain my praises and exhortations about You. Simply put . . . You're the Best!

I adore You . . .

Thoughts to Ponder

1. Have you ever simply thanked God for making you exactly as you are? Martha was good and so was Mary . . . Peter was good and so was Paul . . . Sinners? YES! Yet, God used all of these flawed people and he can use you too. Will you let Him use you exactly as you are?

2. The gifts of the Spirit are: wisdom, knowledge, faith, healing, miracles, prophecy, discernment, tongues, interpretation of tongues. The Bible tells us in I Corinthians 12 that the Holy Spirit gives us the gifts we need as He determines our need for them. Have you ever thought about your spiritual gifts? Do you believe the Holy Spirit will provide them as you have need of them in your life?

Create in me a pure heart, O God,
and renew a right spirit within me.
Psalm 51:10

Good Morning, Abba, Jesus, Holy Spirit,

Amazing God, Holy One of Heaven. Thank You for using me for Kingdom purposes. A flawed vessel, such as I am, You can still take my offering and create good from it! Each new morning You are a source of wonder for me to ponder. I praise You, Father, for the truths that You teach me. You are a God of untold intelligence. Your wisdom surpasses human understanding. You- and You alone -can bring restoration from seemingly unredeemable situations. The most amazing fact of all is that You use *me* as Your hands and feet, as Your ears and eyes and at times . . . you give me words to share. I am eternally grateful for this honor. It humbles me and brings me unrestrained joy.

In the midst of this broken and hurting world, You have placed Your servants; sons and daughters with a mission to be Your hands and feet to serve and to bring You honor and glory. Your eyes are roaming to and fro looking for those who love and honor You, Sovereign Lord. I humbly ask that You create in me a heart, mind and spirit that will cause You to pause in Your search and to say. "Ahh, there is my daughter. She will do *My Will*." How I long for this to be truth, to grow so close to You that I never stray from Your righteous ways.

Teach me Your ways, Lord, and create a right spirit within me. To You will all praise, honor and glory be given. In Your precious name I pray, Jesus.

My honor belongs to You . . .

Thoughts to Ponder

1. We each have a mission. Do you know what your mission is?

2. Look around you and ask God . . . where can I serve? Today is the day to begin a mission with God . . . Will you begin?

*Now may the Lord direct your hearts into the love of
God and into the patience of Christ.*
2 Thessalonians 3:5

Good Morning, Abba, Jesus, Holy Spirit,

I love You, Abba, and Your awe that surrounds me daily. The way that You intertwine our lives for Your purposes is just so very cool. You place us in places for a reason that we may think is just random, but with You nothing is random, everything has purpose. Thank You for being Your amazing and wondrous self.

Oh Abba, I am listening to You and I do see the truth in the necessity of good rest. I also see the reality of three types of rest . . . sleeping, *rest in You, and Sabbath rest.* I am discovering that without regular, sound and adequate sleep, my whole mind, body, and spirit suffers. In the morning, I awaken exhausted and then my time with You suffers. I lose patience at the smallest thing, and I become edgy. Additionally, without *rest in You,* I cannot focus on You and Your plans for me. The lack of sleep and rest in You can become a cycle and so I ask that You would overcome my insomnia and give me good rest. Show me that how I order my day will affect my sleep. Remind me that I need to organize so that I can get to bed at a decent time with a reasonable amount of work having been accomplished. Remind me that I need to set attainable goals so that I am less likely to lay awake because I have so much still left on my list. Abba, I ask YOU to be the author and creator of my list each and every day.

Abba, I do want to talk about the rest we are commanded to participate in: Sabbath rest . . . I find it interesting that many Christians would not dream of breaking most of the 10 commandments and yet are willing to work all day on Sunday. They seem proud of it.

They even brag to their friends, family, and co-workers about how much they got done. Thank You for convicting me regarding this long ago. I look forward to Sunday and resting. By taking a day and not doing things that exhaust me physically or mentally, I find that You somehow give me the time in the week to get everything done. I feel like You create time if we honor You by keeping Your commandments. I am realizing more and more just how deeply I appreciate sitting at Your feet . . . no agenda . . . just "sit" time relaxing in Your presence.

You are my mighty fortress, my Father, my Judge, my Maker, my Abba, my Savior, my Lord and Redeemer; and I love You so.

Come soon . . .

Thoughts to Ponder

1. Regardless of our stage in life a vast number of people in the United States are driven and proud of it. Generally speaking, our physical, mental, and emotional health has suffered greatly from this driven lifestyle, especially our relationships, including our relationship with God. Is it time for you to reconsider rest?

2. Which of the three types of rest are you lacking in your life? Take this challenge . . . for 4 weeks try resting and see if it makes a difference. Be sure to journal daily so you will have a record to look back on.

*And we know that all things work together for good
to those who love God, to those who are called
according to His purpose.
Romans 8:28*

Good Morning, Wonder of all Eternity,

You are, You know, the Wonder of all Eternity! I wish so much that I could invent a new way to help the lost and searching to find You more quickly. If only they knew what they were missing! My life was so aimless before You. You are Purpose-Giver and I love You. Before I gave in to Your Lordship, Jesus, I was angry at everything on the inside but "little miss everything is perfect" on the outside. It is just so wonderful to feel Your peace and joy to my very core. My peace is soul deep at last.

The song "It Is Well With My Soul" explains so much of how I feel. While I have not suffered the tribulations the author of that song did, I have experienced Your gift of "Wellness of Soul." This is a gift available to every single human on earth. Why do so few accept it, Abba? Why is it so difficult to give over bondage and experience freedom? How can we be so easily deceived . . . intelligent people believing wrong is right and right is wrong? Why do I hear the prayer "Come, Lord Jesus, be our guest for this bounty we are about to receive" and then watch those very same people dis-invite You from every area of their lives? Father, open their eyes that they may see You this day. I pray in Your name, Jesus.

All my love . . .

Thoughts to Ponder

1. Can you say, "It is well with my soul?" If you said yes, are you sharing this gift with others? If your response was no, what do you need to ask God to build up within you?

2. When you honestly consider your life . . . have you invited God into every single part of it?

With my whole heart I have sought You; Oh let me not wander from Your commandments! Your word I have hidden in my heart, That I might not sin against You.
Psalm 119:10–11

Good Morning, my Lord and Savior,

You are so generous, Abba. I praise You this morning because You are a God of details! You are my God, and You care for my every need. Bless my friends and family, Abba. Bless each and every one of them with good gifts. Bless them with lives that are honoring to You. Teach all of us to store up our treasures in Heaven and not on this fickle earth.

Abba, I have been thinking about Your commands and here is the thing that is making me crazy right at the moment. This slang term OMG which is of course an abbreviation of saying, Oh my God. Well frankly this disturbs me. What is the deal that Christian's think it is fine to post this on Facebook or use it as part of their vocabulary? You said, "do not take the Lord Your God's name in vain." So do they think that if you just abbreviate it, then it is fine? I am not just complaining. I do have a question about this . . . should I say something? I have asked a couple of people and both of them said don't be judgmental, so I am not sure. Isn't this allowing others to sin against You and maybe they really don't realize it so wouldn't it be helpful? Please give me wisdom regarding this I pray.

This day I ask that You keep our children and grandchildren pure in heart, mind, and body. Father, please do not let them fall prey to the evil one and his destructive plans for their lives. Let them cling to righteousness all the days of their lives. Place devoted believers in their paths each step of the way so that they will not stumble.

Etch Your Word in their hearts and Your truth on their minds. Let deception have NO place in their lives.

Thank You for blessing me, for Your forgiveness, and for second chances.

I love You dearly . . .

Thoughts to Ponder

1. Have you ever thought about the cultural things that we have come to accept as Christians that are actually sin?

2. Do you think we should be silent . . . or speak up when we hear or see cultural norms embraced by our brothers and sisters in Christ?

Draw near to God and He will draw near to you.
James 4:8

Good Morning, Abba, Jesus, Holy Spirit of God,

Is it odd that I long to be in Your presence and yet I have no desire to die anytime soon? I truly long to be done with the battle, sin, and the suffering in this world . . . to trade it in for Heaven's wonder and all that awaits me one day. There is nothing greater than You and the hope of eternal life with You. How is it that I can long so for my homecoming and yet say with all earnest, I am happy and content to be here as well? I have no desire to die, yet I have great desire to be home with You. Perhaps it has to do with what James says in the verse You gave to me today . . . when I draw near to You, You draw near to me and so I am content because You are near me. Yet, because it is You, I will long for more until I am truly face to face with You.

Jesus, face to face with You seems impossible when I think about my sinful nature? How would I ever be able to look into Your eyes realizing the sacrifice You made for me, the cost to You? It seems impossible for me to imagine that I would ever be able to look into your eyes after all You have done for me knowing all the times I have failed You. Sin, it is the great divide, between all that is good and all that is evil. Forgiveness is the great equalizer . . . can mere mortals ever grasp the wonder of what forgiveness truly means for us? See Abba, I think the answer is no. I am not sure we can comprehend the splendor of Your sacrifice for us. In our very best efforts I think we can only accept it as a child accepts the love of a parent after being reprimanded. With heartfelt gratitude we fall into Your arms knowing that all is right with the world once again because You have forgiven us yet again.

Holy God, Righteous Savior, Holy Spirit within me . . . You are all I will ever need, help me to understand Your Word and Your ways evermore clearly in order that daily I will draw nearer to You. I love You and I humbly fall before You in adoration for all that You are and all that You have done for me.

I love You so.

Thoughts to Ponder

1. Do you "feel" the difference when you draw near to the Lord? When HE draws near to you?

2. When we humbly ask . . . HE forgives, period! Do you grasp the truth that there is nothing that can separate you from the love of God?

In the multitude of my anxieties within me, Your comforts delight my soul.
Psalm 94:19

Good Morning, Abba, Jesus, Spirit within me,

Is there anything more stunning than the marvel of Your creation? Abba, I am so thankful for the ways in which I can see Your power. You are so visible in nature; the beauty this morning is breathtaking. Thank You for the bounty of Your creative landscapes on display every morning, always different and always awe inspiring.

My soul longs for the day when I can bow before You with thanks and praises . . . Your plan complete . . . eternal peace and harmony the order of our days. I long for the joy and peace of Heaven. I read David's Psalms and I wonder how it is possible that he can reflect my emotions so well. Anxious thoughts threaten to overwhelm me and yet, it is Your comforts that remind me I am well, because You are with me.

Jesus, thank You for the wonder of Your sacrifice for me. You are a most exceptional Savior in every way, and I praise Your Holy name for all that You are. Give me a sensitive spirit in tune to You and You alone.

No other love compares to Yours . . .

Thoughts to Ponder

1. Do you ever have anxious thoughts that threaten to derail your day? How do you overcome those moments so that you can walk in the freedom of Christ?

2. What is the 'comfort' that reminds you that you are loved by the KING?

Trust in the LORD with all your heart, and lean not on your own understanding. In all your ways acknowledge Him, and He shall direct your paths.
Proverbs 3:5–6

Good Morning, Abba, Jesus, Holy Spirit,
You alone are the One True God. Thank You for Your faithfulness in answering my prayers. Thank You for seeking; family, friends, others I encounter each day, and especially those who are not yet believers. Please, Abba, speak to them in the darkness and the light of day. Morning, noon and night I ask that You pursue them until they make a clear and honest choice. Do not let them hedge or sit on the fence. Please soften their hearts until they become sold out believers in You alone. Show them clearly the difference between believing in the traditions of church and truly having a personal relationship with You.

Correct wrong teaching that may be hindering them from committing to You, Jesus. I love them, Abba, and I know my love pales in comparison to yours. If possible, use me to plant seeds of right thinking within them. I am frightened for them. They must truly think hell does not exist . . . or perhaps it is that "nice guys go to heaven" thing again! I ask one thing: please do not let even one of them perish without giving them a last opportunity to accept You, Lord Jesus.

You are in control, and I will rest in that knowledge for all of my days. True, Righteous God, save Your creation from the evil one's grip. Bring this nation and its people back into a right relationship with You. You are my God, and I am Your daughter, and regardless of the consequence, I pray You will give me the courage to stand for You.

Thank You for Honoring My Prayers . . .

Thoughts to Ponder

1. Do you see the difference between church traditions and a personal relationship with the Lord? What does this mean for you?

2. Does your heart break for your friends and family members who are lost? Do you pray for them? Do you talk to them about your faith?

And now abide faith, hope, love, these three; but the greatest of these is love.
1 Corinthians 13:13

Good Morning, Abba, Lord Jesus, Holy Spirit,

God as man . . . still so amazing and wondrous to me. You were willing to leave Heaven to struggle as we struggle, to feel our weakness and understand our fight against the sin that so easily entangles us. While complete truth, this is just too huge to wrap my mind around; and yet I believe it with all my heart, mind, soul, and spirit.

Jesus, I love You so, and I am so thankful that You were willing to be born to this sad and dying planet so that all of mankind has the opportunity to live for eternity. Today, I am humbly asking that You encourage believers to pursue those You are seeking—with such incredible love—that they cannot help but see the truth of Your message. Abba, bring to our minds moment by moment, throughout our day that we are Your hands and feet . . . that we are Your witnesses . . . and if they do not see You through us, then where will they see You? Abba, I know that technically You don't need us, but I also know that You choose to use us and so I ask that You would use me. Help me to be a witness for You to everyone I meet. Even when I am tired remind me that You must have been exhausted during Your ministry on earth, but you pressed on and so should I.

In all things I trust You, and I place my faith in You and You alone. This is my goal . . . to be in You as You are in me. You are my Savior, Creator, and my Life-Giver; and I am Your devoted child. Make me into one who understands the meaning of a life lived for You.

Make It So, I Pray

Thoughts to Ponder

1. Will you be God's witness to the lost?

2. If not you, then who?

I love the LORD for he heard my voice; He heard my cry for mercy. Because he turned his ear to me, I will call on him as long as I live.
Psalm 116:1–2

Good Morning, My King!

Holy God I give to You my thanksgiving, and praise on this peace-filled morning. Abba, Jesus, Spirit, You are beyond human imagination. You alone are worthy of praise. Thank You for waking me up early so that I can begin this day with You . . . my true love.

Each day, I realize my need of time spent with You. My Bible and You . . . could anything be closer to Heaven? How You have blessed me. It is a good thing that Your gift of Salvation was free of charge because there is no possibility that I could ever do enough to repay You for even this one morning with You.

I can, however, devote my heart, my mind, my soul, and my hands to You and Your mighty work. This is all I have to give, and it is what I give to You this morning. I give You me . . . wholly and completely devoted to You. Abba, as I call upon You this morning I do indeed cry out to You for Your mercy to forgive me for my sins. I ask that on my homecoming day that You will accept me into Your Kingdom through Your Son's sacrifice given for me.

Father, please give a special blessing to Your missionaries across the world who are feeling alone and are separated from family this day. This very day, through Your mighty power, give them a miracle that they have been praying for! Protect them, guide them, bring a bounty of fruit from their labors, I pray.

You are my God, and I will be Yours until my time here ends, and then I will be Yours forever.

I love You so deeply . . .

Thoughts to Ponder

1. Your entrance into Heaven is free of charge . . . ponder that!

2. Consider a mission trip . . . can you go? Can you give money so someone else can go?

*Be anxious for nothing, but in everything by prayer
and supplication, with thanksgiving, let your requests
be made known to God.*
Philippians 4:6

Good Morning, Abba, Jesus, Holy Spirit,

I praise You for all of the protection You provide for my family. You are so good to us and have so faithfully provided for all of our needs and even so many of our wants. Forgive me for not appreciating Your provisions to the fullest extent of my heart. Forgive me when I think I want more. I truly do not need or want anything other than what You provide for me. Remind me of this daily, I pray. Your grace is sufficient for me.

Thank You for constantly molding me and developing in me the skills that can be used for the purpose of building Your Heavenly Kingdom. I do ask that You give me all that I need in order to be a God honoring wife, mother, and grandmother. Please give me a happy heart as I serve my family.

Father, for so many years I prayed for Godly wives for our boy's. Today I thank You for this answered prayer. Thank You that they are now teaching our grandchildren to follow You! Someday I need to write all of the answers to prayer that You have provided but that would take me the remainder of my life and then some. Thank You for choosing me to belong to You. Thank You for giving me a heart and a mind to say yes to Your call. I do love You so!

Thanks to You, my God and Savior . . .

Thoughts to Ponder

1. Once, while on a mission trip, our group encountered a woman alone with three little kids in the jungle. She was incredibly proud because she had built a hut out of mud, weeds, branches, and a piece of rippled metal she found for a roof. There was no furniture but there was a pallet of sorts with a sheet, used for their bed. She had an old treadle sewing machine given to her by the mission church. She was making all sorts of children's clothes from a pile of old jeans she was given. She was grateful, humble, joyful, smart, and industrious. Someone asked her if we could provide more for her and her response has always stuck with me . . . she said . . . The Lord has provided for all of our needs, praise God! She then smiled and said, more thread colors would be nice. I think we wanted to give her stuff to make their life easier . . . she was thinking, more thread so I can earn money to pay for food and to have clean water to drink. The differences between 1st world and 3rd world countries are profound. How do you view your "stuff" and how are you teaching those around you to view 1st world stuff?

2. Are you anxious about anything? Family has been my area of anxious thoughts because I want everyone to have a perfect life . . . yes, I do know that is not possible. I thank God daily for his provisions for my family and for his protection over all of us. Today's verse has been a life changer for me. Now I can let my anxious thoughts simply pass through my mind and not dwell on them. It takes practice! If you are anxious about anything give it a try . . . it works if you allow it to!

*And in all things, whatever you ask in prayer,
believing, you will receive.
Matthew 21:22*

Good Morning, Lord,

I love this early morning time with You; it truly sustains me. To be in sync with You as I begin each day is the greatest wonder of my life. I did not realize what a difference it would make in my heart to spend extended time with You upon waking each day. Mornings with You, Abba, are no longer a "have to" in my life; it has become my lifeline, my heartland, my desire.

Abba, we have entered into a different way of thinking and living in this world of terrorists and hatred. Fear abounds and with it has come the very thing You told us would happen in Your Word; right has become wrong and wrong has become right. Truth has become folly and folly has become truth. It all breaks my heart and so I cannot imagine how it must grieve Yours. Abba, if those who are blinded by the enemy were to read Your Word and see that YOU are Rule-Maker would they change . . . would they fall on their faces and repent? Though we all see through the glass darkly, I know there comes a point where apart from YOU . . . we are totally blinded by evil. Please Abba, bring the blind back from the brink before it is too late.

Holy Trinity, please place on the heart of every person in the United States a yearning for You, and open their eyes and ears to see and hear truth. I pray that the lost souls around the globe would recognize that it is impossible to fill the hole in their soul, with anything other than You. Teach them that You alone are Filler-of-Souls. Awaken Your people and make this a time of revival in this land. Wake up the churches in our country. Impress upon the hearts of pastors that truth is what we must seek. Remind them that they do not need to "sugar coat" Your Word and remind them of Your opinion of a church that is neither hot nor cold. The early church in the book of Acts was power-filled because of their boldness of spirit . . . not because of milk toast sermons that left everyone feeling all warm and fuzzy. Remind us that You are a loving God and You are also a just God. We must teach Your perfect love or the picture we portray of You will be flawed. Let this never be true of me, I pray, Lord Jesus.

In humble adoration . . .

Thoughts to Ponder

1. Does your time with the Lord help you stay strong . . . whatever the day may bring?

2. Do you believe that individual prayers for this hurting world make a difference?

The fear of the LORD is the beginning of knowledge.
Proverbs 1:7

Good Morning, Abba, Jesus, Holy Spirit,

How I long to sit at Your feet, to hear the angels sing, to listen to the stories of Your power and majesty, to kiss the feet of my Savior, to touch Your face, to simply *be* in Your presence, Holy God.

Daily, I am amazed that You chose to create me, to seek me, to save me, to invite me to be Your daughter . . . daughter of the King Most High. I adore You, and, as usual, I have no adequate words to express my love for You. In You alone I am complete.

I love You far more than this world. Do I still concern myself with the things of this world? Yes, I do. Some of my concern is warranted, but some of it is self-serving. I ask Your forgiveness for this fact. I would like to say that I never fall prey to the enticement of the world, but I do. The world is fading for me, but I have so far to go until I am truly "in this world but not of this world." Help me to realize quickly when I am focused on myself and stuff instead of on the lost and suffering. I pray.

Create in me a heart so huge that others see that I am different and ask why. Then give me ample words to speak of Your love for us . . . and our need for You. Give me knowledge and wisdom like Solomon but also the heart of David so that I will not fail You. Help me to finish strong.

I pray You will make it so.

Thoughts to Ponder

1. What are some of the things of this world that still entice you?

2. How are you doing with keeping your focus away from self-serving thoughts?

*Hear, O LORD my righteous plea; listen
to my cry. Give ear to my prayer—it does not
rise from deceitful lips.*
Psalm 17:1

Good Morning on this day of revelation!

Thank You, Abba, for men and women of God that You clearly speak through with Your power on display! Martha Horn was one of those women. I cannot imagine the dance she is doing with You today, she communicated Your love and truth so beautifully while on this earth. Thank You for her and thank You for the legacy of her life . . . communion with You is all that truly matters.

It is in the living of everyday life in communion with You that matters. When we resist the world, as hard as that is, You fill our thoughts and You are willing to speak through us. Please, Abba, make my thoughts Your thoughts and Your ways my ways. My truest desire is that I will "walk with God." This is what You did, Jesus. You were so in tune with the Father that His ways were Your ways. You were fully human, and so it is possible to do this! We cannot be sinless because of course we have sin within us and we must deal with the sin on our doorstep that so easily entangles us. We can however, as fully human as we are, remain connected to You, moment by moment and day by day.

I humbly ask for Your strength, wisdom, and love; and in doing so, I ask that I will find a depth of Spirit so compelling that it will become contagious to every person I encounter.

I love You so completely . . .

Thoughts to Ponder

1. Is your truest desire to, "walk with God"? Can you imagine what our world would be like if more Christians truly desired this?

2. Are you in communion with God? Look at the synonyms for the word communion before you answer!

*I can do everything through Him
who gives me strength.
Philippians 4:13*

Good Morning, My First Love,

I praise You for being a personal God. You are not only God Most High; You are also Abba . . . Daddy. That is almost to amazing to even write. The fact that I can crawl up in Your lap and just talk to You, finding security, peace, and grace . . . there are no words to tell You how much that means to me.

Jesus, thank You for making possible this intimacy with You, Lord. I would have been satisfied with simply touching the hem of Your royal robe, but You offered me everything! You offered me the key to the throne room and to the best Daddy in the universe. You offered me a Brother who was willing to lay down his life for me. Even more amazing than that, You gave me the very heart required to accept Your extraordinary gift. In You, I find my comfort and salvation, and I am deeply grateful.

Holy Spirit, help me to be sensitive to Your leading every moment of every day. Help me to keep my house in order for the coming storms. They will come and I know this. Please prepare me, by Your mighty strength, to handle anything that comes my way. Remind me that the storms are simply another way to make me more like You, Jesus. Since You suffered many storms, surely I will also. Remind me daily of Your strength.

I love You . . .

Thoughts to Ponder

1. Today simply bask in the love of the Lord . . .

2. Enjoy being HIS!

And those who are Christ's have crucified the flesh with its passions and desires. If we live in the Spirit, let us also walk in the Spirit. Let us not become conceited, provoking one another, envying one another.
Galatians 5:24–26

Good Morning, Lord God, Holy Savior, Spirit,

Your creation is so beautiful. When the sun shines on the snow, the sparkle is breathtaking! Thank you for giving me such beauty to behold.

As I read Your Word, I discover new and wonderful things about You and realize that it is very hard to be just like YOU. Forgive me for the nails I have pierced You with. This walk with You is much harder than I imagined it would be nearly 40 years ago when I became Your daughter. I want to live righteously, yet I fail time and again! I get grouchy, I am selfish, I want things to go smoothly, to go "my" way, and I get angry sometimes when they don't.

Help me to take my day's moment by moment, to confess when I mess up but to move on! Allow me to begin fresh this moment. Lift my spirit, I pray. I desire to be useable, moldable clay. Lord, turn me inside out that I may know all that stands between us. Search me, cleanse me, renew me, I pray in Your name, Jesus. Teach me how to be more like You each day. You are praiseworthy, and I love You.

Loving You . . .

Thoughts to Ponder

1. Have you ever wondered why Christians often tell others that if they accept Christ everything will be easy? This walk is incredibly hard . . . being a Christian is not popular in these dark days. There are some that watch my life just waiting to find inconsistencies they can point out to me. So why do you follow Christ? I know my answer . . . what is your answer?

2. Having answered the above question of why you follow Christ, what is your greatest stumbling block to being a great example for others?

Blessed is every one who fears the LORD,
who walks in His ways.
Psalm 128:1

Good Morning, Abba, Jesus, Holy Spirit,

I love You so much, and this morning time is so vital to our relationship. I simply cannot get through my day without beginning it with You. Abba, as You well know I am so easily distracted and it doesn't take much before my mind starts wandering. Help me to remain focused on You and the message You have for me each new morning.

Today I feel as if I have been thirsting, and right now I am at the well drinking my fill. You amaze me. You know what I need before I do . . . how to solve my problems . . . even what my struggles will be. My need for You grows daily. Please . . . never lift Your mighty hand from my life.

Thank You for being my God, my Savior, my Light in the darkness of this fallen world. I am humbled by Your grace and Your unconditional love for me. Thank You that You always provide a way of escape when I am troubled. Help me to recognize "my escape" when it comes. I see the long path I have yet to travel, and I am awed that You will be faithful to keep me on the road of righteousness as long as I keep my focus on You. Guide each step I take, I pray.

You are the One I love . . .

Thoughts to Ponder

1. Have you noticed a difference in the way your day goes when it begins with the Lord?

2. When you find yourself in a tough spot do you remember to ask God for your way of escape?

It is the Spirit who gives life, the flesh profits nothing.
The words that I speak to you are spirit, and they are life.
John 6:63

Good Morning, Abba, Jesus, Holy Spirit of God,

On this gorgeous morning I praise You for who You are! Awe is to simple a word to describe my amazement that You have always been and will always be. Truly, I cannot wrap my mind around the concept of *"Always."* Yet, I do not doubt it for a moment. For me, it is an absolute fact that I simply do not understand because of my limited capacity for eternal thinking. Everything about You is life-giving. I can feel my spirit respond and awaken when I read Your Word, when I listen to You, and when I praise You.

Forgive me when I lack faith in certain areas of my life. You know those things which are beyond difficult for me . . . my husband and our children! Watching our kids in painful situations or seeing them struggle with something that they must walk through . . . something I cannot fix for them. Remind me that I cannot fix things for anyone. I cannot even fix myself . . . only YOU can. Abba, You know how I struggle when I have for some reason disappointed my husband or the kids . . . worrying for days that they will never forgive me for letting them down, but knowing in my heart that I will again and again because I am a flawed human. Teach me how to forgive myself. It is so easy for me to forgive others but so hard for me to give myself grace. Thank You for Your "renewing faith" which captures my heart day after day. Jesus, You are too incredible for words. Thank You for being my Savior.

Bless this day I pray. Give me a clear mind for Your purpose. Keep me ever mindful that it is You and You alone doing Your work through me. My hands and heart can do nothing of eternal consequence without You. Bless this family, create a love for You in each of us that will sustain us in both the brightest and darkest of moments, I pray.

You alone are worthy . . .

Thoughts to Ponder

1. What is harder for you, forgiving yourself or others? Why do you think it is so hard?

2. How often do you speak life into others? Have you ever considered speaking scripture over those you love?

I will extol You, my God, o King; and I will bless Your name forever and ever. Every day I will bless You, and I will praise Your name forever and ever.
Psalm 145: 1–2

Good Morning, Dearest Lord and Savior,

Oh, how my heart softens at the very thought of You. You give me a peace like no other. As I look out my window, the beauty of Your creation brings a tranquility that comes from You alone. I love You so, and I am deeply grateful for my blessings . . . already too numerous for one lifetime.

Abba, if today were my last, my only regret would be that I wasted so many long years serving the world when I could have been serving You, my Maker, my Father, my King. Father, you are the beginning of me, and You are my end. In You alone will my spirit yield and find peace. How I long to bow down before You, to touch You, to see Your shining glory, to behold my Savior.

Abba, today I am thinking of the mighty work You have done in our children. I see them growing into men of God right before my eyes and I am amazed that You gave them to me to steward as their mom. I know that it is You at work in them that creates a heart for You and nothing I have done. I cannot even take credit for praying for them, because it is YOU that gave me the heart to pray! They belong to You, not me and You are creating something beautiful within them and I am thankful.

I love You and I praise Your Holy Name this day. Please allow me the humbling honor of serving You until my homecoming arrives. Allow me to bless the lives of those around me.

I love You more than any other . . .

Thoughts to Ponder

1. If today was the last day you had on this earth what would you do?

2. What does your answer to question one tell you about your relationship with God? With others?

*Be anxious for nothing, but in everything by prayer
and supplication, with thanksgiving, let your requests
be made known to God.*
Philippians 4:6

Good Morning, Abba, Sweet Savior, Spirit within me,

Jesus, I feel like we need to have a serious talk this morning. The Trinity is (as You know) hard for me to understand. Because it is hard for me, I get this concern that borders on worry about my prayer focus. All of my prayers (written and spoken) I address to all three of You. Yet, I talk to You, God more than to You, Jesus. It says in the Lord's Prayer . . . Our Father . . . and since You, Jesus, gave us that model, it is my basis for prayer. However, it also says that no one comes to the Father unless he has come to the Son and that is the rub. Is it even possible to offend You in this? I see You ALL as one . . . yet, as Christ my Savior, as God the Great I Am, and Holy Spirit as the guiding force within me. All of this to say . . . my heart is pure, my love is genuine, and I do my best to walk with You. If I am missing something critical, bring it to my attention and follow it up with solid teaching from Your Word.

Jesus, I hate my pocket full of nails. I do not want to ever hurt You again; my record is long enough . . . Heaven has endured enough sin done by me. Cleanse me. I desire to be pure, holy and clean before You. How many times will I cause You the pain of taking on my dirty filth? Forgive me, Lord, Savior, Lion Of Judah, for both the huge and microscopic sin in my life . . . including that which I know I did and that of which I am not even aware.

Help me to be more like You this day. I love You with all my heart. Bless me for Your purpose.

Love and honor to You . . .

Thoughts to Ponder

1. What are your thoughts in regard to how to address the Lord in prayer? Have you ever thought about it before?

2. How do you view your sin? I have encountered many people who think they are somehow less sinful than others because they are 'pretty nice' and they try hard to 'do good things.' God says that sin is sin . . . what is your response to that?

For the LORD takes pleasure in His people; He will beautify the humble with salvation.
Psalm 149:4

Good Morning, Abba, Jesus, Holy Spirit,

Where are they now, Lord . . . each life that has intersected with mine? Where is my eternal perspective? If I viewed life with Your eyes, would I choose to live even one day as I have? What am I doing for the lost and hurting of this world? Oh, I love to serve You, but how much really? How often am I willing to serve beyond comfort? Have I really counted the cost . . . picked up my cross and served . . . really served? Sometimes I wish You didn't ask me these really tough questions. Yet, on the other hand, I am so happy that You do. On these days, You help me to see two truths. The first truth is this . . . I am making progress. The second truth is harder . . . I have a long way to go. Every time I am about to pat myself on the back, I am brought to my knees once again by a lost opportunity for eternal purposes. I am reminded once again that an eternal perspective is the *only* perspective that You care about!

I give to You all my praise, and You alone are deserving of praise. I ask that You give me eyes that see as You see. Please do not let me miss those in need this day.

Jesus, I love You for being my teacher . . .

Thoughts to Ponder

1. Do you think you view the world with an eternal perspective?

2. Does your 'to do' list interfere with doing what you hear God asking you to do? Does fear ever stop you?

Ask, and it will be given to you. Seek and you will find.
Knock and it will be opened to you.
Matthew 7:7

Good Morning, Abba, Jesus, Holy Spirit,

My true and forever Love . . . that is who You are! I ask that You do a great work in my heart, and You are faithful to do just that. I stand amazed that I have changed in attitude so quickly. Is it possible that one day I will be an example for others to follow because I so fully live for You? That would truly be a day of great joy for me . . . to overcome that which is in this world. I know that it is YOU, Jesus, who makes me able to do just that. The key is . . . what I know as "head knowledge" needs to become heart- changing, action- based living! Please make it so!

Bless my relationships with peace, joy and understanding of each other, I pray. Please allow love to overcome my past sin and serious mistakes in parenting, friendships and marriage. Help me develop Your wisdom and knowledge by growing my heart and desire to lean on You and never on my own understanding.

Give me the heart and tools I will need to be Your servant each and every day. Expand me for Your purposes, I pray. Please overcome the evil that hurts this world . . . our wounds are so deep, and there are so many who do not understand that You and You alone are the Great Healer.

You are my One and Only . . .

Thoughts to Ponder

1. What does 'action-based living mean to you?

2. Where do you need a 'heart change'?

How lovely is your dwelling place, O LORD almighty!
My soul yearns, even faints, for the courts of the
LORD; my heart and my flesh cry out for the living
God. Psalm 84: 1–2

Good Morning, Holy Father, Son, Spirit,

It is very difficult some mornings to choose just one of Your traits to center my praise on. This day I choose to praise You for every single, wonderful trait that makes You my Creator, my God and my dearly beloved Abba.

Jesus, thank You for Your sacrifice that made it possible to be cleansed from my sins. I desire to come before You every morning, clean from a fresh washing by You, the One and Only, able to cleanse me completely. Forgive me for testing You foolishly at times. I don't know what gets into me to decide (without the benefit of prayer) to do some of the things I do.

Abba, thank You for Your Holy Spirit who gently whispers truth into me, or gives me a nudge when I am getting off track. I love it when I am mentioning some issue to You, and a creative solution enters my head, one that I would never have thought of. On occasion, You do have a BIG thing to say, and I hear it loud and clear . . . but for the most part, You speak to me through Your Word and prayer. I am thankful for the way You speak to me, I remember when I desperately wanted You to do great signs and wonders through me, or give me lofty messages to share . . . now it makes me laugh or ashamed . . . kind of like the Sons of Thunder issue I suppose. Now I see the beauty in what we have. You have helped me understand that humility is always good for Your children to embrace with appreciation.

I truly adore You, and I am just so thankful for Your ownership over this life You breathed into me. Abba, help me get beyond the discouragement I feel when I am misunderstood by others. I have a quirky personality and I hesitate to say things I probably should . . . and say things I probably should not. However, I would never say anything to intentionally hurt or wound anyone, especially someone I love. Teach me how to say the things I should and seal my lips when I need to be silent. Lift me up, I pray, through You, my Brother Jesus.

Just because You ARE . . .

Thoughts to Ponder

1. How does God speak to you? When are you most able to truly hear Him?

2. Do you allow God to have true ownership over your life?

A word fitly spoken is like apples of gold
in settings of silver.
Proverbs 25:11

Good Morning, Wondrous Trinity!

My praises for You this day are abounding. Each day as I grow closer to You, Your voice is clearer. I prayed for encouragement, and You gave me an entire rainbow of reasons to be encouraged! What a Mighty God You are. Your promises are true yesterday, today and tomorrow; and that is all I need to know.

Abba, lately I have been thinking about the church as a whole. Since we are Your temple we are each individually a part of the church and collectively we are the entirety of the church body. As a church, You call us to be beacons of truth, peace, union, wisdom, forgiveness, and love. There is no room for holy huddles or gossip in the guise of "sharing for prayer." If we are not truly inclusive of all, who will be shunned? How many have turned from the church because they felt excluded or judged? I am not sure most would like to see those numbers.

We are called to spur one another on to love and good deeds while coming along side our weaker brothers and sisters. Aren't we each weaker at times and stronger at others? Isn't it a given that we will switch roles depending on the circumstances we find ourselves in? When we complain about, talk about, or exclude anyone, aren't we doing that to You?

Help each and every church become a body of health and vitality! Give us the will and the desire to include new people in our old circles. Remind us to be silent when we should and to tame our itching tongues. Teach us Your ways, Jesus and show us our sinful ways in order that we might confess and change. When the time comes for each of us to reach out to the lost, give us the courage and boldness to do so.

Bless this home and family, I pray. Keep us from harm. Give wisdom and discernment to each of us that we may serve You more fully. Change us, mold us, and keep us within Your protective will this day.

I love You so dearly . . .

Thoughts to Ponder

1. When thinking about yourself at church, are you part of a holy huddle? If so how can you begin to break it up? Do you want to?

2. If you are more of a loner, how can you begin to reach out to others? Do you want to?

Better is one day in your courts than a thousand else-
where; I would rather be a doorkeeper in the house
of my God than dwell in the tents of the wicked. For
the Lord God is a sun and shield; the LORD bestows
favor and honor; no good thing does he withhold from
those whose walk is blameless.
Psalm 84: 10–11

Good Morning, Abba, Jesus, Holy Spirit of God,

I praise You, Jesus, for the transforming work You have done in my life. I praise You with everything that I am. Thank You for releasing us from; guilt, shame, and self -pity. The freedom available to us through Your redeeming work on the cross is profound in every way! Abba, if we are willing to read Your Word, open our hearts and our minds, You will take our lives and breathe the very life of Christ into them. I am forever grateful to You for teaching me that it is only when I walk in the spirit that I can overcome the darkness of my soul. It is through Your Spirit within me that I find victory!

Father, I desire to walk in the flow of Your Spirit all the days of my life. It is Your Spirit within me that removes the blinders from my eyes, and allows me to see Your truths. I feel so intimately connected to You with Holy Spirit filled eyes. You are so completely cool! I love You, heart, mind, soul *and* spirit. I am filled with a love so wondrous that there are no words left to speak.

Thank You, Lord Jesus . . .

Thoughts to Ponder

1. What transforming work is happening in your life right now?

2. Are you living in the freedom that Christ gives to us?

With my whole heart I have sought You;
Oh, let me not wander from Your commandments!
Your word I have hidden in my heart,
that I might not sin against You.
Psalm 119:10–11

Good Morning, Most Loving Awesome Lord,

I have such joy in my heart and soul even with all of the problems of this world. You are Peace-giver and Heart-settler, and I praise You and give You thanks. Thank You, Abba, Jesus, Spirit, for simply "being" and for loving me.

I love to think about how You created each of us . . . unique . . . yet in Your image. To imagine that one day before the foundations of the earth were laid that You, The Great I Am said, "Today I am going to make this child. I will give her blue eyes and light brown hair, and she will love to smile! Then, in all of Your awesome wonder I was created just as You designed. That makes me feel so incredibly special . . . not proud . . . amazed by You and Your creative wonder. Abba, I am delighted every moment of every day that You are my creator and also my Father.

It is such a beautiful day; I do so enjoy Your creations. I pray that today I may touch hearts and spirits for You. I desire to be a lifter of Your Holy Name and of my brothers' and sisters' spirits. Mold me and make me into useable clay. Make my path straight and keep me focused on Your holy path.

I ask Your blessings on this family and our efforts to honor You in all of our ways. Give us the strength to stand strong in the coming days, whatever they may bring.

I love You so.

Thoughts to Ponder

1. Have you ever taken time to thank God for loving you before the foundations of the earth were laid?

2. Today, memorize Psalm 119:11, *Your word I have hidden in my heart that, I might not sin against you.* This verse helps me to remember daily what makes me useable for God's purposes . . . a cleansed heart and a clear understanding of God's Word.

*In the multitude of my anxieties within me, Your com-
forts delight my soul.*
Psalm 94:19

Good Morning, Abba, Jesus, Holy Spirit within,

I am once again humbled and grateful for Your pro-
vision for this family. Your Spirit moves within me in a
tangible way, guiding me to function as You would have
me. Oh, how I desire for this to happen at all times!
Thank You for everything, for a lifetime of blessings, a
loving family, wonderful children and a happy marriage.

Abba, as You know better than anyone I am struggling with exhaustion again. I know that it means I am
trying to do things in my own strength again. Forgive
me when I take over and decide I can do more than
You've asked of me on any given day. Remind me to
ask YOU for my list of tasks for the day and when the
list is completed to stop and rest. I will need Your help to
make positive choices through this foggy brain. Give me
right and kind words with all I meet this day. Housework
overwhelms me when I get tired like this, please help
me accomplish what needs to be done. Remind me
that a regular, early bedtime is vital to the ministry You
have given to me. Please strengthen me this week, put
me to bed early and allow my body, soul, and spirit to
rest in You.

You are my rock, my comfort, my strength, my salvation. I love You more than any other . . .

Thoughts to Ponder

1. What is your on-going physical struggle? I have struggled with bone aching exhaustion for years. In the Bible, Paul, had an issue with his eyes, Moses, stuttered . . . we learn from reading our Bible that physical issues are to be used for God's Glory . . . to show that we can do nothing in our own strength. Have you talked with God about your struggle and how it can be used for His Glory?

2. What step is God asking you to take to better manage your physical struggle for His glory?

And now abide faith, hope, love, these three;
but the greatest of these is love.
1 Corinthians 13:13

Good Morning, Holy One, Name Above All Names,
   Abba, You are all powerful and I adore You. You can change a heart in the blink of an eye, yet You give us free will. I will never cease to be amazed by You. I truly desire to have a heart like Jesus. To have a heart like Jesus is how I desire to choose to exercise my free will, to be like You, Jesus, all the days of my life.

To turn the other cheek and mean it!
To give and love unceasingly!
To serve others with total joy!
To abide in my Father always!

   What an agent of change for Kingdom purposes I would be if these traits of Yours would become traits of mine, not some of the time, but all of the time!
   My heart explodes with joy at the thought of one day bowing before Your throne . . . the throne of the One True Majestic God! O Lord, please send Jesus for us soon. Help me to do my part to bring every single person possible into the Kingdom. There are just so many who still need to know You.
   Keep me strong for the battles to come. Teach me Your word and make me a warrior mighty in the battle. Protect me from the flaming arrows of the enemy with the shield of my faith. Jesus, teach me to be like You; help me, Spirit, to live within the will of my Father; show me the way moment by moment, I pray.

With my tender love for You . . .

Thoughts to Ponder

1. Is there anyone in your life that you need to forgive? Is there anyone you need to love unconditionally or pray for without ceasing?

2. Do you serve others with total joy?

Keep your heart with all diligence,
for out of it spring the issues of life.
Proverbs 4:23

Good Morning, my Sweet, Sweet Lord,

I praise You, LORD, for Your perfect plan. You alone are the meaning of perfection—not the counterfeit that the enemy tries to deceive us with. The only true perfection is that which You bring about or what is found in Your creation such as a wild flower that grows from bud to full bloom and then re-seeds itself for the next summer season of life. Please allow me the wisdom to walk within Your plan for my life. Keep the enemy far from me and remind me that I must listen to You alone.

Jesus when You were here . . . and because You we fully human, did You have conflicting emotions regarding Your purpose? Did You ever just want to take a nap and forget about the multitudes of people outside Your door? Did You ever think . . . I have so much to do today, Abba-Father just let me rest . . . and we will have a longer time together tomorrow? Yes, I do know the answer from Your Word. If You needed rest, You rested, because the work was too important to not take the time to rest. After all, the will of Your Father was at stake. You show us in Your Word that You rested in Your Father, spiritually, emotionally, and mentally . . . and when possible, You rested physically too.

Thank You that through Your Word I can see that this time with You each morning is the source of my energy. After a full night of prayer with Abba, You did Your most amazing work. Remind me whenever I need it; that awakening early for our time together will give me strength and keep me alert . . . not strip it from me. Perhaps the most important reminder I need is that time spent with You is never wasted. You have shown me time and again that when I order my day with You first . . . I never cease to be amazed at how much we are able to accomplish.

I see more and more the importance of balance, Your balance. Just as You did not heal every hurt, in every town, I too must choose my service wisely. I know that the wisdom of choosing correctly comes from an intimate relationship with You Abba. Make it so, I pray, in Your name, Jesus.

I love You . . .

Thoughts to Ponder

1. Do You see Christ as the source of your strength and energy?

2. Do you make a regular bedtime a priority so that you are able to awaken to spend time with the Lord?

*I have hidden Your word in my heart
that I might not sin against You.
Psalm 119:11*

Good Morning, Abba, Jesus, Spirit,

Thank You for the warmth of this home and for our abundant blessings far beyond my knowledge. Listening to the rain and wind this early morning makes me think of the homeless in our country. Abba, protect them, give them shelter, I pray. If You want me to have a role in changing this national epidemic impress it upon me and show me my next step.

You are mightier than the greatest army and more loving than any other. You are more generous than the widow who gave her last two pennies and more fearsome than the most ferocious lion. Again, I sit amazed that You created me, loved me, and came seeking me to make me Your very own. That is far too large to wrap my tiny mind around, but I will cherish the truth it contains all the days of my life! Forgive me for not spending enough time just marveling at the wonder of You!

Thank You for warmth, children, music, rain, life . . . Thank You for the blessings I don't even know about. Thank You for Your grace and mercy, for forgiveness, for blue skies and rolling clouds. Thank You for Your constant care for me, for my brothers and sisters in Christ, and those who are coming to You soon! Remind me often that I, too, was lost and You never gave up on me. Let my diligence be constant as well! Please continue to refine me so whatever circumstances I find myself in . . . I will remain part of Your remnant . . . and led by Your heart.

I will joyously love You forever . . .

Thoughts to Ponder

1. Are there local needs or national issues that you think about often? If so, perhaps God is asking you to serve in some capacity in this area. Make today the day you take 10 minutes to look into how you might serve others . . . and please God by doing so.

2. How concerned are you for the lost? What can you do to turn your concern into Great Commission action?

Great is the LORD and most worthy of praise, in the city of our God, his holy mountain. It is beautiful in its loftiness, the joy of the whole earth. Psalm 48:1–2a

Good Morning, Giver-of Good-Gifts,

O Lord, You are so worthy of praise! Spring is amazing! It refreshes the landscape, and it refreshes my soul and spirit. What a creator You are! Everywhere I look, there is another amazing creation. You are the One True Genius, the One True Master Artist, Scientist, Doctor, Inventor and Lover of My Soul. O, how I love You, how I long to listen to Your words of wisdom. O, how I long to sit at Your feet and worship You, my Master, my Lord, my Maker.

Show me, guide me and teach me according to Your word, I pray. I desire to be a servant with a humble heart. Remind me that I must serve with the heart of Mary and the gusto of Martha . . . that would truly be a great combo! Abba, I kind of wish that there was not a gender assigned to the story of Mary and Martha because it truly applies to male and female. I am surrounded by male versions of the Mary and Martha story. Men too can be Mary or Martha in the way they respond to work and worship.

This day I pray for the ministries that do so much for the Kingdom. I realize that is a rather large prayer because there are so many. Bless them, Abba; bless them indeed. Expand their territories for Your purposes and keep them safe from harm. To You, Great King, I give my praise this day.

All my Love . . .

Thoughts to Ponder

1. Are you more of a Mary or a Martha? What is a step you can take to increase the traits of the one lacking within you?

2. Are you praying for your local ministries? What a great service that would be for them!

*But thanks be to God! He gives us the
victory through our Lord Jesus Christ.
1 Corinthians 15:57*

Good Morning, Abba, Jesus, Spirit,

Forgive me, my Lord. You called to me in the night, and I chose sleep over You. I feel such deep regret. I know I lost something I cannot replace. Forgive me in Your name Jesus. The worst part is that I asked You to get me up so that we could be totally alone, and You did . . . yet, I chose sleep over time with You. Here I am again, trying to walk that line of obedience. I honestly don't know what is with me sometimes! I am so grateful that You never give up on me and that You are always waiting to forgive me and to give me one more try. The victory is always in You alone!

I praise You, sweet Lord Jesus. You alone are right and true and good. I am so deeply grateful to have You for my example. Daily, You give me good food from the Word; and You are always close to pick me up, dust me off and cheer me on once again.

Today, while a bit sad for failing, I still have a deep desire to get back on target. I thank You once again for Your faithful forgiveness.

You are the life within me . . .

Thoughts to Ponder

1. Have you ever asked God for something and then ignored His answer? Why do you think you ignored the answer? Did it require something from you that you were not ready to give?

2. Obedience is difficult on our best days and seemingly impossible on our worst days. What helps you the most when you are struggling to be obedient to God's Word?

You were taught, with regard to your former way of life, to put off your old self, which is being corrupted by its deceitful desires; to be made new in the attitudes of your mind; and to put on the new self, created to be like God in true righteousness and holiness.
Ephesians 4:22–24

Good Morning, Abba, Jesus, Holy Spirit,

It is 3:00 A.M., and I bow before You and am amazed that once again You have given me a second chance! I praise You Holy God Most High. You have called me to pray, but for whom?

O, Abba, how is it possible that this nation could fall so far from You in just over 200 years? When will this nation learn? Open the eyes of every man, woman and child, I pray, Jesus. Our eyes need to be opened to Your ways and truths . . . I ask that You will make it so. This nation must seek Your face and repent of the multitude of sins we have committed, for surely time is growing short.

Holy Spirit, I do not even have the words to pray for this nation. I do not have the wisdom, discernment or the knowledge needed. I am struggling for understanding. I ask that You take over every part of me . . . mind, body, soul and spirit. Take away my worldly ways and replace them with Your righteousness, I pray. Create within me a new spirit that is filled with Your light. Make me a useful vessel so that the work I do is Kingdom worthy. Use me, but please never let it be me that others see. I desire that You alone shine through me. Every time You humble me I see how far I have yet to travel. How can I help others if I have so far to go myself? The answer is so easy and so hard . . . by putting off my old self and putting on more of You. This can be the day I do just that. Please make it so!

In my Saviors name I pray . . .

Thoughts to Ponder

1. What are the issues we are facing as a nation that burden you? Do you pray for a God honoring change daily?

2. Often I realize that I need to "put off" another part of my old self . . . such as my tendency toward being an introvert. What are the things you need to put off . . . what will you put on in their place?

Whenever God slew them, they would seek him;
they eagerly turned to him again. They remembered
that God was their Rock, the God Most High
was their Redeemer.
Psalm 78:34–35

Good Morning, my King, Savior, Spirit Most Holy,

Speak to me my Lord! Bless me with wisdom, knowledge and understanding in these dark days. I desire to serve You and spread the Good News to this world of darkness, a world that is masked with false light . . . the light of the evil one who truly masquerades as an angel of light, just as your Word says. When the mask finally falls away, I ask that You save Your faithful remnant from harm. Whether that means that You bring us home or that You cloak us in Your protection, I beg You, Lord God, have mercy on Your people. Save us in these times of trouble. Remind us that we have Your peace no matter what we may be experiencing, I pray in Jesus Name.

I ask that You take charge of my thoughts, my actions and my deeds. Spirit, I invite You to not only dwell within me but to fully consume me. I want to be a fire for You, Lord God! Guide my every thought. Bless me with a heart overflowing with Your fruit.

Create matching hearts in Your children . . . interchangeable with one another and one with Your Spirit! Let us praise You in harmony. Let us worship You as one body, one mind, one spirit. Mold our wills to match Your will, I pray. If needed, teach us what that means. Today and forever I give to You praise and glory!

I love You my King . . .

Thoughts to Ponder

1. How different would your life be if you were fully con-
    sumed by the Holy Spirit?

2. Have you ever thought about how different our wit-
    ness to the world would be if we let go of our petty
    differences regarding how we "do church" and
    instead worshipped with one heart and one mind
    . . . i.e. focused on our praise for our Mighty God
    instead of our personal preferences?

Those who live according to the sinful nature have their minds set on what that nature desires; but those who live in accordance with the Spirit have their minds set on what the Spirit desires. The mind of the sinful man is death, but the mind controlled by the Spirit is life and peace.
Romans 8: 5–6

Good Morning, my Lord and Savior,

Your blessings never fail to leave me in awesome wonder! All praises belong to You and Your boundless goodness. I deserve not one whit of what You do for me, and that makes my blessings all the more incredible! How joyous to go to sleep in Your care and awaken with thoughts of You on my mind!

My heart cries this morning for the lost and hurting of this world. They have been blinded by evil, Abba. How You must weep for them! I am so sorry that Your beautiful creation—man, made in Your very likeness—has turned against You. If even I, as limited as my vision is, can see truth, why can't the majority of the world? When will You finally say *"enough!"* When will Your mighty hand of judgment fall and declare that we have gone too far?

My joy is that I know from Your word and from Your character that You will save Your faithful remnant. I pray that future generations will see our arrogant and prideful ways and be repulsed by them! I pray that as our children grow, they will say that surely there must be more than this . . . and in their search they will find You! Forgive us, Abba, in Jesus' name for leading generation after generation astray. We have truly done evil in Your sight. Bring us back to righteousness as a people and as a nation I pray in Jesus' name.

I love You . . . let my life reflect this . . .

Thoughts to Ponder

1. If our nation doesn't turn back to God . . . what is your view of the future? What are we leaving to the coming generations?

2. I see two thought processes in Christians today . . . which mindset do you hold . . ." Things have always been like this, look at the Roman empire, now is no different"—or—The time is short, we need to work diligently for the purposes of the Lord? What is your Biblical backup for either mindset?

In the same way, the Spirit helps us in our weakness.
We do not know what we ought to pray for,
but the Spirit himself intercedes for us with groans
that words cannot express.
Romans 8:26

Good Morning, Abba, Jesus, Spirit,

I love You. Each day that You give to me is a tender mercy. You are our Life-Giver. If You lifted Your hand from me for even a heartbeat, could I do more than exist? Never are You absent from me, never removing Your protection over me, or failing to keep me in Your loving care. Thank You, Abba, for so many years of Your mercy, love and protection. Thank You, Jesus, for being the Rock of my salvation, for without You no mercy would be possible.

I have been so burdened lately for the collective sin of our nation. I don't even know what to pray anymore, yet I do know that the best thing for me to do is PRAY! I will plant, water, and harvest as You direct . . . and pray that the harvest will be great . . . and soon. In my own heart, I need to be ever true. If my witness is weak, I can do nothing for others. Remind me that my course must be straight at all times.

Today, I ask for Your protection on my true family . . . those who believe in You, Jesus. Keep them from spiritual harm. Strengthen Your children, Father, and bring us closer to You each day. Refine us and use us for Your purposes and glory. Allow us to be servants that are true examples of You Jesus . . . every day. Create in us a—stand apart—quality that intrigues those around us and makes them say, "I want some of that!" And when they come to us, let Your Word pour out from our lips and extol the wonder of walking with You! Holy Spirit, when I have no words left, when I fail in even knowing how to pray anymore, I ask that You intercede for me.

All my love to You . . .

Thoughts to Ponder

1. What area of your life needs refining? Are you willing to work on this?

2. Do you 'stand apart'? Do you want to?

The angel said to the women, "Do not be afraid, for I know that you are looking for Jesus, who was crucified. He is not here; he has risen, just as he said. Come and see the place where he lay. Then go quickly and tell his disciples: 'He has risen from the dead and is going ahead of you into Galilee. There you will see him.' Now I have told you."
Matthew 28:5–7

Good Morning, Mighty God, Beloved Savior, Spirit within me,

It is Easter Morning and I am overwhelmed by Your goodness to me. Jesus, here I am ready to do my devotions, and I look outside my window and I see three crosses as plain as day. We have been living in this new house for four weeks and I have been sitting in this very spot looking out that very window every single morning and I have never noticed them. Yet, this morning I awakened kind of sad (after watching the video of the doctors giving the medical rendition of what You went through on the cross) so I was just sitting here looking out my loft window. I looked out the window and noticed first one, then two and then the third cross in plain sight! I was overwhelmed with joy and thanksgiving because the cross is empty and Your suffering is over forever! You have given me a reminder of what You have done for me that will with remain with me for as long as I live. Yes, I know they are power poles but from here they are crosses in perfect formation for me to remember what You did and I am humbled . . .

I pray for pastors the world over this morning. Abba, Jesus, Holy Spirit, give them the strength, the courage, and the boldness of spirit to preach Your Word in truth and grace. Bring the lost into Christ-centered churches this morning and let them leave as new brothers and sisters in Christ! Remind those surrounding them that they will need to be discipled because following You is not for the weak of heart. Give these new believers the strength they will need to turn from their old ways and to seek the wonder that is found in You.

Joyous Resurrection day to You my Risen Lord. Thank You for Your gift to mankind, forgive us for not appreciating it as we should. Truly, this day I sit in Awe of YOU, my Risen King.

I love You completely . . .

Thoughts to Ponder

1. 'He has risen from the dead and is going ahead of you into Galilee. There you will see him.' Do you see HIM? You will if you are truly following Him!

2. If you had been God's sole creation do you believe Jesus would have gone to the cross for only you? The answer is yes, he would have. You are that special to Him—so live like it!

My salvation and my honor depend on God;
he is my mighty rock, my refuge.
Psalm 62:7

Good Morning, my Beloved Lord,

I praise You for all things. I will easily praise You for the positive things, but I also praise You for the trials that You ask me to go through. That isn't quite so easy, but it is a critical element in my walk. I must learn to be thankful for everything that comes from You for my growth, even when it hurts.

Having said that, Abba, I need Your reassurance more than ever. I don't want to lose my extended family, yet I know that if I press to far, they may reject me. Where is that balance between being a witness and being a pain in the neck? I have a hard time finding it. I am sad that You are a forbidden subject and that if I show my adoration for You, then I am considered a freak. It hurt me so badly when I heard the words: "we are just worried that you are taking this religious thing to a bit of an extreme." First of all, I am NOT religious, I am in love with You. Secondly, it is not possible to carry my love for You to an extreme. Frankly, I don't think I have even scratched the surface of the love You deserve.

Today, I feel like a broken vessel. You are the potter, and I desire to be the clay that You bring up from the miry pit, and then center it on Your wheel to make something beautiful. Could You remold me with right ways and words that will heal and never wound? There is such power in our words! Remind me of this fact daily, I pray in Jesus' Holy Name.

Hold me in Your loving arms this day . . .

Thoughts to Ponder

1. Are there things in your life that are hard to praise God for? Can you do it anyway?

2. How do you feel about standing out . . . versus . . . fitting in? What does God's Word have to say about it?

In his hand are the depths of the earth, and the mountain peaks belong to him. The sea is his, for he made it, and his hands formed the dry land.
Psalm 95:4–5

Good Morning, Maker of the ocean breezes,

Blessings and all praise to Heaven this wondrous day. I want to tell You how looking out at this beautiful ocean affects me. The warmth of the sunshine You have given me reminds me of the breath of my babies when they laughed while I kissed them . . . warm, milky, joyous, soothing, a complete stress reliever. Just as my babies brought such peace to me, so does this living canvas of Your awesome creativity. Total peace envelops me . . . mind, body and spirit. You are peace-giver and the apple of my eye. As the ocean breeze brushes ever so lightly over my face and arms, I wonder . . . is this what angels' wings feel like? The sound of the surf softly roars in the background of this masterpiece as ever so slowly the world awakens around me. I can hear the seagulls soaring above me, calling their praises to You for this glorious day. Thank You, Abba, for these gifts of nature at this moment untarnished by man.

Thank You for this awesome gift. I will treasure these memories in my heart. Today I ask that those who live here will look out at this and see it as I do. Please remind them that this is a unique gift each and every day.

In awe of You . . .

Thoughts to Ponder

1. Where is that one place . . . so magnificent . . . that you simply must stop and praise Him?

2. Bask in HIS creation today . . . and thank Him for it!

Blessed be the Lord, Who daily loads us with benefits,
the God of our salvation!
Psalm 68:19

Good Morning, Great and Glorious King!

What a very great day this is! This morning could easily be the most glorious on earth today. I have always loved the sounds of the beach . . . the roar of the surf so mighty and powerful, the cry of the ocean birds soaring in the salty breeze. The chatter of the people always muffled, relaxed and soothing- as they walk by. This is extraordinary . . . Thank You! What a contrast to Michigan in the throes of winter. I love the majesty of winter, but it is truly a gift, an honor and a privilege to experience the wonder of both. The beauty and the beast . . . warmth and sunshine today, bone-chilling cold tomorrow . . . mercy and wrath. Could I truly appreciate one without the other?

I long for Heaven, where the climate, the landscape, the relationships . . . well absolutely everything will be perfect. We will be perfected and in Your presence forever. This truth . . . of what we have waiting for us is too wonderful to grasp.

Once again, You have blessed me beyond reason. Forgive me for not seeing Your handiwork every moment of the day . . . even in winter back home. Give me Spirit-filled eyes to see the beauty of this world, in nature, people and, most of all, You!

I love You so.

Thoughts to Ponder

1. Mercy and wrath . . . think about this today.

2. Do you long for Heaven?

It is for freedom that Christ has set us free.
Stand firm, then, and do not let yourselves be
burdened again by a yoke of slavery.
Galatians 5:1

Good Morning, my King,

Abba, this spot where I spend my morning time with You has taken on a special quality to it. Each time we have moved I have struggled to find "our spot" but this time I just knew the moment I stepped into this space. This is where I can be absolutely alone with You, to learn from You, listen to You, talk to You, and tell You how much You mean to me. Thank You for this place.

I praise You for the treasure You hide within me each and every day by Your Holy Spirit. Thank You for giving me eyes to see these nuggets of wonder, keep me humble and contrite in order that I will never take a moment of this for granted. Please keep me from self-absorption because that would mean missing out on the most supernatural of moments with You. You are freedom Jesus . . . As long as I keep my focus on You, I am free and nothing in this world can enslave me ever again. For me, this freedom is profound and worthy to praise You for . . . forever.

Today, I choose to walk with You, Jesus. I choose to listen to You, Holy Spirit. I choose to increase my knowledge of You, Father, by reading and studying Your word. I choose to serve You by serving those You place in my path. I choose this day to demonstrate my love for You by following righteous ways. I make these choices because You gave me the freedom to do so . . . and that is the coolest truth of all!

Come soon I pray . . .

Thoughts to Ponder

1. Do you realize that the way you respond to every single event in your life is a choice?

2. If you are in Christ . . . you are free . . . no chains can hold you now.

Create in me a pure heart, O God, and renew a
steadfast spirit within me.
Psalm 51:10

Good Morning, Precious Savior,

You are more precious to me than anything in this world. I say this . . . but is it true? I have plenty, and so it is easy for me to say that stuff doesn't matter . . . but what if I didn't have any stuff . . . a home, food, clean clothing, and warmth . . . then what would I say? When I have been on mission trips I have seen the exuberant love devoted Christians of third world nations have for You and it overwhelms me with wonder. They have nothing of a material nature but because they have You, they have all they need. Would I feel the same? Striped of everything would I still love You the way I do today? These were the questions Job faced weren't they Abba . . . he passed, would I? Frankly, I don't want to find out and I pray that You will keep me from the sorrow of Job. Yet, I have to say, thy will, not my will be done. Our nation is in deep trouble Abba, and so I may live out the remainder of my life in third world nation conditions and if this should come to pass, give me the strength to remain in You. I humbly thank You that for now I can sit . . . surrounded by the beauty of this amazing world— yet one in the throes of death—a world both joy-filled and sorrow-filled . . . yet I find no conflict with this state of affairs as I know that You Jesus are on the throne.

I pray that I will be steadfast for all the days left to me!

I love You so.

Thoughts to Ponder

1. What do you think about what is written above?

2. Amazing beauty and horror co-exist on this earth . . . I look forward to the day that horror is gone forever.

For there is one God and one mediator between God and mankind, the man Christ Jesus, who gave himself as a ransom for all people. This has now been witnessed to at the proper time.
1 Timothy 2:5–6

Good Morning, Abba, Jesus, Holy Spirit,

I am sorry for these tears, but they are tears of joy. I give You my thanks and praise. I pray that each of Your children will fall in love with You more each new day! There is no better way to live than secured within Your loving arms. Please continue to grow my heart for the lost and hurting, by growing my heart for the things that matter the most to You. May my love for You bloom into larger and larger blossoms of joy and service. I desire to know You so intimately that when You breathe a breath, I adjust my course to match. Forgive my sins, Sweet Savior Jesus. Make me pure before my Father, by Your cleansing blood. This sacrifice You made for me . . . giving Your life for me, being beaten and tortured for me . . . how can it be? Perfect man, given for sinful man, there are no words—ever—to give thanks for what You did for me, I love You so.

Thank You for watching over me . . .

Thoughts to Ponder

1. Are you secure in our Father's loving arms? He wants you there desperately, run to Him today!

2. He gave Himself for you . . . isn't that too wonderful for words?

We always thank God for all of you and continually
mention you in our prayers. We remember before our
God and Father your work produced by faith, your
labor prompted by love, and your endurance inspired
by hope in our Lord Jesus Christ. For we know,
brothers and sisters loved by God, that he has chosen
you, because our gospel came to you not simply
with words but also with power,
with the Holy Spirit and deep conviction.
I Thessalonians 1–5

Good Morning, Abba, Jesus, Holy Spirit,

Abba, how amazing is this passage, how much clearer could it be? You tell us, without any doubt, that there is more to salvation than *words* . . . You say: "[4] For we know, brothers and sisters loved by God, that he has chosen you, [5] because our gospel came to you not simply with words but also with power, with the Holy Spirit and deep conviction." You tell us with complete clarity that we are loved by YOU . . . actually chosen by YOU, and when the gospel comes to us—the work of Jesus while on earth—his life, death, and resurrection, we react passionately. That moment, when we first believe, is one of raw emotion expressed in dozens of ways. The moment when we declare as Truth Your sacrifice for us is impossible to describe; but it is a realization of YOU and YOUR reality, and we believe!

Therefore, we are saved, right? Well, yes, but Abba, I need to talk this through with You because there has to be a reaction beyond that initial emotional response. We need YOUR power, which comes from Your Holy Spirit, and with that power comes deep and abiding conviction. Abba, I can have an intense emotional response to a lot of things but does it move me to change my life? See that is the crux of the matter isn't it? Did I change?

Did this decision to follow You change my very DNA in a spiritual sense? The answer to this question of "change" must be yes! However, if everyone answered yes, then why is our Christian country now a "post-Christian" country when 75% of the people still claim they are Christians? I realize clearly that we are all fallen creatures so we all sin daily, but so did the early church and they changed the world! Abba, I would like to consider this more tomorrow . . . it is a deep topic that I want to spend today pondering with YOU and then talking more about. The next part of this passage seems very key in grasping true belief.

I love You Holy Trinity, I desperately need more of YOU growing within me. It is when You consume me that I am able. Apart from You, I fail so much and so fast it scares me. Apart from You I am just a fallen human in the flesh. With You I am victorious and full and Holy Spirit filled with joy as my banner of hope for a new day.

Abba, my prayer for this family is that in all things and in all ways we will each bring glory to YOU. I pray that YOU will continue to bless us with the abundance of heaven and that we will be witnesses for YOU out of that abundance. I pray that it will be a good harvest today and that we will each do our parts to make that so.

I love YOU and pray all things in and through YOU Jesus . . .

Thoughts to Ponder

1. Have I allowed The Holy Spirit to change my spiritual DNA?

2. Have I truly become a New Creation in Christ Jesus?

You know how we lived among you for your sake. [6]
You became imitators of us and of the Lord, for you
welcomed the message in the midst of severe
suffering with the joy given by the Holy Spirit.
[7] And so you became a model to all the believers in
Macedonia and Achaia.
I Thessalonians 1:5–7

Good Morning, Abba, Jesus, Holy Spirit,
Thank You for a wonderful quiet morning. I love sitting here listening to the rain on the roof, it is a special treat for me. Thank You. Abba, I am grateful for Christian friendships. It is so nice to spend time with people who understand YOU! These things are all so amazing and good and special to me. It is astounding to me what You give to us each and every day; the generosity of Your Spirit is beyond human words to describe. People are consumers of everything and, apart from You, we offer nothing of value to this world. One thing I am realizing this morning is the value of friendships that are centered on You. Spending the evening with Christian friends was immeasurably good for me and I am humbled by this gift You provided for me. I needed to laugh and to know that I am loved by friends.

Abba, I am still thinking about this passage: "These people became imitators of the disciples and of the Lord . . . with joy . . . in the mist of suffering" (1 Thess. 1:6). I looked at the synonyms for imitator and I found; copycats or clones. A clone is an exact replicate or to be genetically identical to its ancestor. I think that is significant to realize that many people were able to look at the life of the disciples and the message of Jesus Christ and change completely into imitators of Christ. What is even more amazing is that these people were not living in a comfy community with likeminded people, great healthcare, plenty in every way. No, it states that they did this in the midst of suffering! Yet, this passage also tells us they had joy! Joy is not happiness; it is that bubbling up of an infectious faith of knowing all will be well. Joy is a statement of heart that says regardless of circumstances I have a peace that cannot be thwarted . . . because You are my God and I am Your child. Do people see this in me? Is this an obvious trait in the United States Christian church? Do we see infectious faith, joy, imitators of Christ surrounding us? We have everything in this country . . . even the poorest among us are rich by world standards. Where is our joy, where is our Christ Identity . . . where is mine? The downfall of this nation is coming quickly . . . perhaps the blame can be found in us. I need to spend more time thinking and talking this through with You.

I love You and I thank YOU for this day. Bless us I pray and keep us in Your loving care as You have every day since our birth.

I love You so.

Thoughts to Ponder

1. Do people look at you and see an imitator of Jesus Christ?

2 .Do you have infectious joy?

Final Thoughts . . .

If you are reading this page it means one of two things . . . you are like me and flipped to the last pages first or you made it through your first three months of journaling! I would like to end my part of this journey with you in the same way we began . . . with a few questions . . .

1. What makes God special?

2. Why do you love Him?

3. Could you lose your love for Him? If so, how and why?

4. Do you enjoy spending time with God? Why?

5. Do you believe God enjoys spending time with you? Why?

6. Could you have this special loving relationship with the Lord without investing time into it?

7. How has this journey strengthen your relationship with the Lord? Has this helped you create a lasting bond with Him forever?

8. Do you believe this equation: Time Invested = Depth of Love in your relationship with the Father, Son, and Holy Spirit?

9. How has your experience over the past three months changed you?

10. Will you continue to journal with the Lord?

I pray the answer is a resounding YES!

CPSIA information can be obtained
at www.ICGtesting.com
Printed in the USA
FSOW03n2236021016
25672FS

9 781498 477994